Queen Elizabeth II in the robes of
The Most Noble Order of the Garter
Photo: Thomas Mace-Archer-Mills.

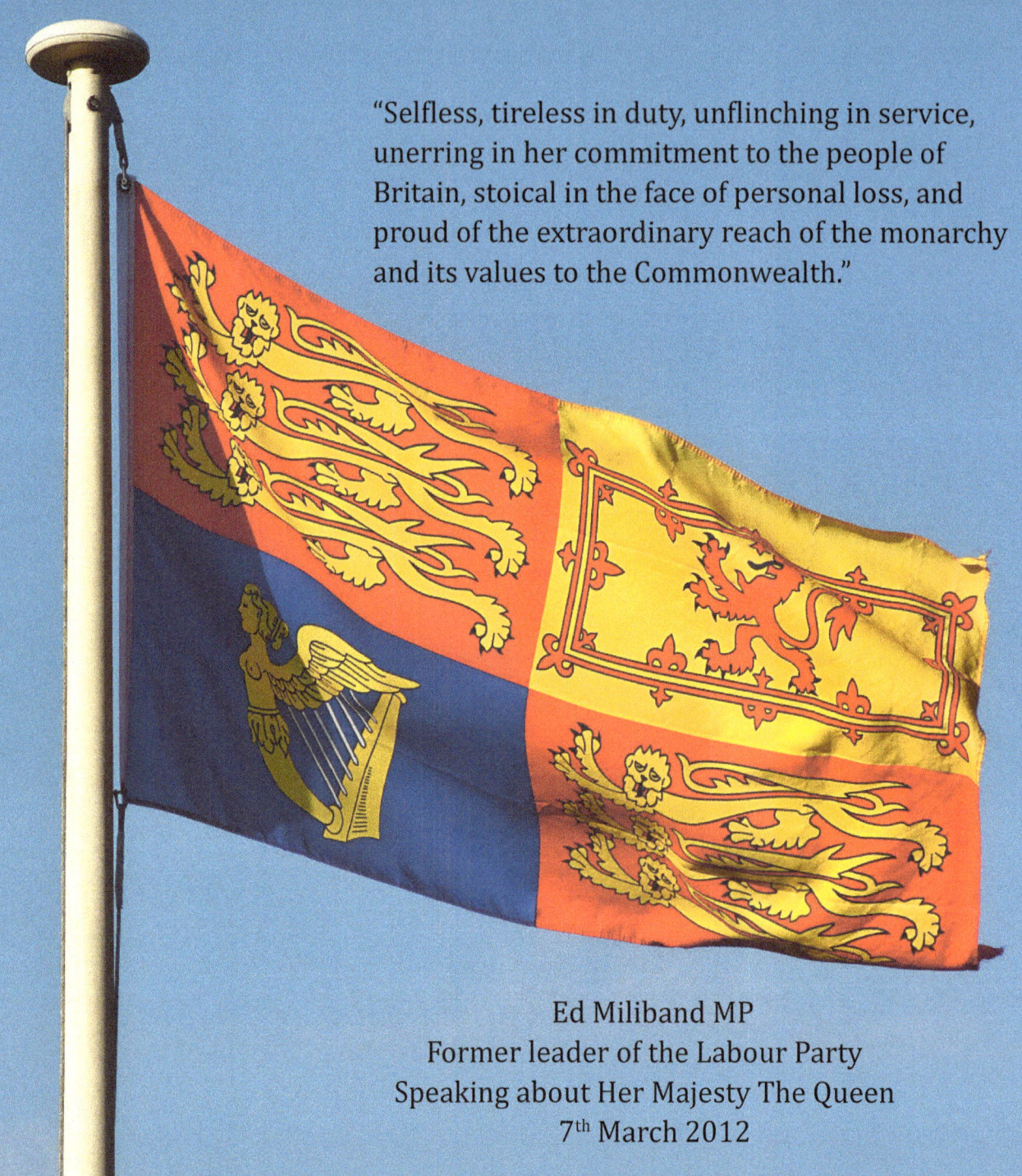

"Selfless, tireless in duty, unflinching in service, unerring in her commitment to the people of Britain, stoical in the face of personal loss, and proud of the extraordinary reach of the monarchy and its values to the Commonwealth."

Ed Miliband MP
Former leader of the Labour Party
Speaking about Her Majesty The Queen
7th March 2012

Their Majesties' Mixers

"When They Reign, They Pour."

by

Thomas Mace-Archer-Mills

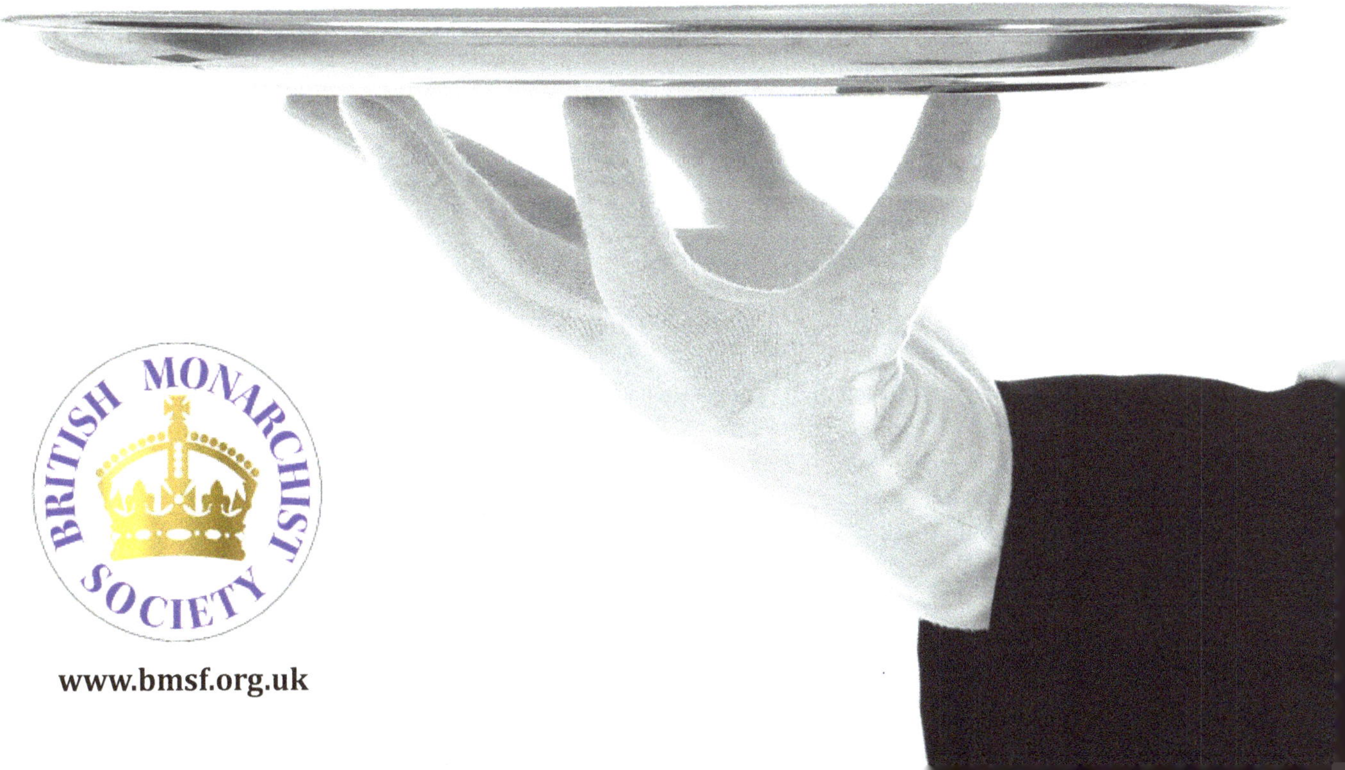

BRITISH MONARCHIST SOCIETY

www.bmsf.org.uk

Published by
Filament Publishing Ltd
16 Croydon Road, Waddon, Croydon,
Surrey, CR0 4PA, United Kingdom.

On behalf of British Monarchist Society
www.bmsf.org.uk

© Thomas Mace-Archer-Mills 2019

Second Edition
ISBN 978-1-912635-53-5

The right of Thomas Mace-Archer-Mills to be identified as the author of this work has been asserted by him in accordance with the Designs and Copyrights Act 1988.

All rights reserved. No portion of this work may be copied in any way without the prior written permission of the publishers.

Cocktail photography courtesy of Michael Champion.

NOTES FOR THE READER

The recipes in this book use both metric and imperial measurements. Follow the same unit of measurement throughout; do not mix metric and imperial.
1 teaspoon = 5 ml. 1 tablespoon = 15 ml. 1 fl oz = 30 ml = 2 tablespoons.
Recipes using raw or lightly cooked eggs should be avoided by the elderly, pregnant and breastfeeding women, infants, convalescents and anyone suffering from illness.
Please consume alcohol responsibly.

Dedication

We raise a glass to Her Majesty Queen Elizabeth II, for being our anchor in times of turbulent seas, the great builder of a vast and complex network of international unity, and the steadfast and resilient constant, which has kept her people and lands bound together in friendship, brotherhood and common unity. Here is to the longest reigning British monarch in history, to whom not only these sceptred isles and territories have witnessed, but the world has respected, learned and matured from.

Thank you for your lifelong dedicated service to your people around the world, and for always being a beacon of hope and continuity when the world has needed you most. We would not be where we are today if it were not for your guidance, care and courage.

God Save The Queen!

Acknowledgements

My little Britton – Always follow your dreams, no matter how big or small you imagine them. Strive for gold, but do not be disappointed with silver, bronze or a number. The most important aspect of your life is acknowledging that you have given an honest and true effort with the best of your abilities. You are much loved and most treasured.

Those in my world who have departed to a better life, free from hardship and worry, to watch down over me and guide me on my lifelong path. Goodbye is not my finest moment; however, the lessons taught, and the help afforded, have made me eternally grateful as your blessings still come to shine upon me. You have touched and shaped my life, and for that, my success is yours. You are always close in my heart and mind.

~ Special Thanks To ~

My families for always being supportive, believing in my dreams and steadying me when I stumble.

Grandfather George – the most loyal and dutiful Grenadier Grandfather I know. Thank you for affording me such a fine "Royal" education all these years.

Mummy, Anthony, Granny Mervyn, Valerie, Adam, Penny, Mike, and Eugenie, without whom I would not be so blessed in family, friendship and support.

The M Family of Restaurants and M-Den – Thank you for the countless evenings of inspiration, research and creation. By far the best bars and luxury lounges in London!

Table of Contents

Foreword by Sir David Amess MP	9
Introduction by Andrew Rosindell MP	13
Prologue by Thomas Mace-Archer-Mills	17
A Royal Mixology	33
A Royal Line Up - Cocktails by Lorenz Tullio Santonocito	63
From Her Majesties' Kitchen - Chef Robert Kennedy	121
Royal Canapés	122
A Right Royal Tipple	135
Windsor by Royal Proclamation	151
Their Majesties' Mixers - The ANGOSTURA ® Story	159
Royal Brandy Drinks	175
Royal Champagne Drinks	191
Royal Gin Drinks	211
Royal Rum Drinks	245
Royal Scotch Drinks	261
Royal Vodka Drinks	277
Royal Whisky Drinks	289
A Royal Finale - Liquid Desserts	307
About the Author - Thomas Mace-Archer-Mills	327

The Round Tower, Windsor Castle.
Photo: Thomas Mace-Archer-Mills.

Sir David Amess
Member of Parliament for Southend West

Royal Family is not something most people would think of doing. However, the subject itself, when properly examined and researched, is quite interesting and historic. The topic blends modern British culture with the historic origins of the consumption of alcohol in the early days of British life. From the ancient kings of old, to Protestant Sovereigns taxing spirits imported from Catholic nations, to the favourite tipples of The Duke and Duchess of Cambridge, *Their Majesties' Mixers* is a unique blend of Royal authority, social trends and modern pastimes which all relate to the distillation and consumption of spirits in Britain over the years. Wine, mead and ale were common drinks throughout our history, when alcoholic beverages were a safer alternative to the often polluted and infected water supplies available at that time.

Many cities, such as London, during the medieval era drew their drinking water from the rivers and streams within the Thames tributary, which were heavily contaminated with bacteria due to the lack of a sewerage system. I should, at this point, add that the constituency of Southend West, which I represent, lies alongside the Thames Estuary. Some areas of the country enjoyed water from clean streams, but the majority of the people favoured the alcoholic alternative, which was cheap and widely available. Today, we take clean water, as we turn on our taps, for granted, but it was a very different matter all those years ago.

The Crown represents the living history of this nation. Our sovereign is only the latest representative of a monarchy which spans almost a thousand years. I have always been a staunch royalist. We are the envy of the world because in contrast to Presidents, our Queen is above party politics and is the rock on which our State is built. I have had the good fortune to meet Her Majesty and other members of the Royal Family on a number of occasions, culminating in my own investiture at Windsor Castle in 2015. On every occasion, I have never failed to be impressed by the grasp that The Queen has of how special such a meeting is between "subject and monarch".

An enormous amount of research has gone in to the production of this book about "Royal tipples". The background of each Royal subject, the times in which they lived and the particular beverages they favoured, make up a fascinating story. I have found it an absolute pleasure working with Thomas, as a Core Patron of the British Monarchist Society and Foundation. I have the highest regard for the organisation, which is dedicated to celebrating the rich tapestry of life that the monarchy brings to all of us. It was a childhood ambition of mine to become a politician and a Member of Parliament. How well I remember witnessing my first State Opening of Parliament as an elected Member. Words are insufficient to adequately convey to the reader how wonderful the pageantry surrounding Her Majesty's arrival is, but it is not just a show. It, in every sense, symbolises how the various organs of state are entwined to underpin that which we all hold dear, our democracy.

It is often said that we, the British, certainly know how to put on a show and I have often observed how tourists are absolutely smitten with the wonderful discipline of the Household Cavalry as they arrive with Her Majesty's State Coach at the heart of the procession. History is dripping out of this book (no pun intended). Thomas has provided a fun, interesting and historic way to illustrate how alcohol has played a large role in the history of not just the kings and queens of this nation, but the people of Britain as a whole. To learn that "Mother's

Ruin" (Gin) was heavily influenced by King William and Queen Mary as a cheap Protestant alternative spirit to the costly imports from Catholic nations, further underlines the direct connection between our Royal forefathers and the drinking public.

My tastes are simple. I like a good dry white or "rich red" wine, good quality port, a "whisky mac" (whisky and ginger ale) and, of course, champagne, over which countless conversations with Thomas have been had. We have in common the desire to create and capture history and to document it for the enjoyment of others. We also make history. As a Member of Parliament of some three decades plus, my bound copies of Hansard are testimony in themselves to how history is shaped. So, it is then, that this book is also making history. It is the first of its kind, a "Royal tipple". I hope you enjoy it.

Sir David Amess
Member of Parliament
Southend West

Andrew Rosindell
Member of Parliament for Romford

The importance of Her Majesty The Queen to Her Realms and Territories is outlined through a relationship which for decades has been built on trust, leadership, example and the bonds of brotherhood. Although 2017 marked the 100th anniversary of the House of Windsor, the greatest milestone of The Queen's reign was taking her place as the longest reigning sovereign in British history, and now her Sapphire Jubilee of 2017, the result of a journey which has touched the most remote corners of our planet, to which her story and her milestones are the result of what remains of "the great Imperial family, to which we all belong". The sun may have set on the British Empire, but something unique and valuable remains: the Commonwealth. Out of the Commonwealth's 53 nations in total, 15 have remained loyal to the Crown which has served them as faithfully as the day Princess Elizabeth became Queen. However, one, on the other hand, which makes up Her Majesty's 16th realm, is a true testament to the power, nature and political cohesiveness which serves the people: constitutional monarchy.

Her Majesty's realms are unique in many ways, but most importantly for blending their unique cultural characteristics with the deeply seated and valued Crown, of which Her Majesty is Head of State. The bonds between the

The flag of Papua New Guinea.

realms and Her Majesty are strong, as they are built upon the lifelong service, dedication and work that Her Majesty has continued to provide since the day she was crowned. Papua New Guinea as Her Majesty's 16th realm holds a very interesting and special place within Her Majesty's realms, for it is the only realm which was not inherited. Upon obtaining independence from Australia in 1975, Papua New Guinea found itself in a position somewhat complicated. A newly independent nation comprised of over 1,000 tribes with over 800 spoken languages, the country found itself in a position of tribal partisanship in which forming a government with a neutral Head of State was impossible.

The solution to this problem was one that would solve many of the nation's problems and provide a solid and secure footing for the nation to advance and thrive; invite Her Majesty The Queen to become the Head of State of Papua New Guinea. Her Majesty graciously accepted to become Queen of Papua New Guinea, which the nation would become a realm upon joining those already in this unique category such as Antigua and Barbuda, Australia, The Bahamas, Barbados, Belize, Canada, Grenada, Jamaica, New Zealand, The Solomon Islands, St. Christopher and Nevis, St. Lucia, St. Vincent and the Grenadines, Tuvalu and the United Kingdom.

Being a nation which democratically invited a "God-anointed sovereign" to become the monarch of an independent nation, Papua New Guinea is the youngest constitutional monarchy in existence. The ideals and values held by its people, that a Head of State who is above politics would, and has, helped unite the people of Papua New Guinea, whilst allowing the nation as a whole to come of age in a modern and industrial world. Papua New Guinea has been able to rise above its tribal differences to become one people under their Queen. With the stumbling block of social division removed, this nation has seen rapid growth, economic development and prosperity under Her Majesty The Queen over the past 40 years. The examples set forth by her, along with the care, consideration, loyalty and duty to her people within the nation has proven in a widely republican world that sometimes the binding of people together through an ideology above politics is the best form of government which truly provides for its people in various ways.

The term "provide" is a word which possesses many different examples within it. From The Queen, to The Crown, to the nation of Papua New Guinea itself, this is a realm which has been well provided for by the institution of what Her Majesty represents – a collective voice and will of the people. In a period of celebration, Papua New Guinea also carries on its legacy by bearing witness to milestone events in 2015 such as Her Majesty becoming the longest reigning sovereign in British history, her life's work celebrated as the Commonwealth celebrated its 50th anniversary, her realm of Papua New Guinea celebrating its 40th anniversary and the birth of her great granddaughter, Princess Charlotte.

No milestone is complete without a celebration and what better way is there to celebrate the reigning monarch of the House of Windsor, than raising a glass to properly toast the health, dedication and continued reign of The Queen?

This book is a unique and interesting way to outline not just your own celebrations during this most historic year, but to learn about the history of spirits and the Royal Family through the generations. Each reader will take away many different points of interest from the content ranging from Royal canapé and cocktail recipes to Royal history, anecdotes and quotes of The Queen and even a brief history of the realms, which the reader may not know. Thomas has created a wonderful tribute to the House of Windsor, Her Majesty The Queen, the Commonwealth and beyond in a style which is all his own. After thoroughly enjoying his earlier publication which celebrated Her Majesty's Diamond Jubilee in 2012, this book is sure to delight, enthral and capture the reader in a fun and celebratory way, whilst paying tribute in a uniquely alternative way to the House of Windsor and the lifelong service of The Queen to her people.

Andrew Rosindell

Andrew Rosindell
Member of Parliament
for Romford

Prologue

by Thomas Mace-Archer-Mills

This compilation of "Royal" drink recipes is enhanced by a mixing of quotes, fun facts, canapé recipes, drink recipes and fun instructions to celebrate the times in which we live. Times to which we are witnessing true history in the making. There are not many books which look at the inside of a Royal liquor cabinet, let alone the favourite tipples and drinking habits of the Royal Family. It is this fact, along with the contents of this book, which are paired to create a truly unique and specially blended book experience to celebrate not just the birth of baby Sussex in 2019, a new baby Cambridge and the wedding of HRH Prince Harry, both in 2018, the 100th anniversary of the House of Windsor in 2017, but the Mother of our nation and her historic 2017 milestone in not only becoming the longest reigning monarch in British history but the only monarch to ever celebrate a Sapphire Jubilee; a woman who is near and dear to many the world over. It is on our ships at sea, in our outposts around the world and at our dinner tables at home, that the familiar and endearing toast "The Queen!" has been followed with nothing less than a spirit of our own choosing. As if becoming the longest reigning sovereign in our history is not enough, the Commonwealth to which Her Majesty has devoted her life has come of age as new children have been added to the family. The Commonwealth of Nations has celebrated 50 years of its existence, all measured, managed and nurtured by the invaluable statesmanship given by our Queen, Elizabeth II.

The Royal House to which Her Majesty belongs has given the world some of the greatest monarchs it has seen in the modern era. Queen Victoria reigned over approximately a quarter of the world's population and a land mass equivalent in measure. She was Queen and Empress of the world's largest empire and the foremost global power which still reigns supreme today as the world's most influential nation in terms of soft power. Though she was of a different Royal House, her heirs and successors would continue to build a great nation throughout the years, albeit with a very different but quintessentially British family name - Windsor. Inheriting the responsibilities of and sharing in many of the same burdens as his mother, King Edward VII produced one of the longest running and brilliantly crafted stage shows the world has seen: the British Royal Family. King Edward was adamant that the Royal Family be the fabric, unifying factor and key focal point of this United Kingdom, where he would build a fabulously decadent stage to produce this fantastic and majestic brand of popular productions. The Mall, Admiralty Arch, The Victoria Memorial and Buckingham Palace itself, with its intricately decorated rooms of white, cream and gold, along with its iconic balcony (first introduced by Queen Victoria), were created and redesigned as great props to keep the Royal Family the focus of the nation and in fact the world for decades to come.

King Edward's son, King George V, led the United Kingdom through the perils of the "Great War" whilst renouncing and abandoning his family's German roots to create the Royal House of Windsor, the House by which the British Royal Family would come to be known. King George V is known as "one King with two houses", abandoning the House of Saxe-Coburg and Gotha (Sachsen-Coburg und Gotha) and creating the House of Windsor to quell any notion or rumour that the Royal Family was not "British", but rather German during the First World War. King George V faced the dark clouds of war not so much with other nations, but with members of his own family, such as his cousin, Kaiser Wilhelm of Germany. The King's other cousin, Czar Nicholas II of Russia, appealed to him directly in the face of imminent danger during the early days of the 1917 Russian Revolution.

The Czar hoped to be granted sanctuary for himself and the Russian Royal Family, but it was not to be. King George V denied his cousin's request on the advice of his advisors who argued that it was important for the survival of the monarchy, that The King distance himself from his Russian cousin. His Majesty received devastating news that his cousin the Czar and the Imperial family had been murdered along with their servants in Yekaterinburg on 17th July 1918, one year to the date that George V, by proclamation, changed the name of his Royal House.

Buckingham Palace.

Edward VIII rode the wave of prosperity that his father King George V cemented after the Great War, whilst enjoying his elevated and popular stardom status as a "Royal celebrity" and "playboy Prince" before meeting American divorcee Wallis Simpson. His subsequent relationship with this woman would plunge the House of Windsor and indeed the nation and former Empire into a constitutional crisis. With a reign of 326 days, Edward is one of the shortest-reigning monarchs in British history. Eventually choosing love and self over duty to Crown and Country, Edward was never crowned King and abdicated his rightful place on the British throne to his brother George VI in favour of a Parisian mansion filled with pugs, memories of a Royal life discarded, the title "The Duke of Windsor" and a wife who would never be styled "Her Royal Highness".

As if the Abdication Crisis of 1936 was not enough of a strain on King George VI, his battle with a stubborn stammer and countless public speaking engagements would be the least of his worries. The clouds of war soon began to cluster on the horizon, which would see a full attack on Britain, its people and the House of Windsor during the Second World War. Leading his people through the darkest days of the Blitz and the subsequent years which plunged Britain into devastation, recession and rationing, King George VI was a triumphant monarch.

A much-loved sovereign with a very popular Queen behind him, he proved to both the nation and the world that Britain would emerge from the black veil of war to become the steadfast and inclusive leader of a reconstructed and unified Empire. So influential and popular was the House of Windsor, that one of its greatest assets during the War forced Adolf Hitler to declare that Her Majesty Queen Elizabeth (The Queen Mother) was indeed "the most dangerous woman in Europe". Defying Nazi bombs and remaining in situ at Buckingham Palace, despite it being bombed over nine times during the war, King George VI and Queen Elizabeth rallied the nation and its people to "Keep Calm and Carry On". Together as a family, the Windsors would be the role models for a scared and threatened nation which needed them so desperately.

King George VI died unexpectedly from cancer while his daughter, Princess Elizabeth, was undertaking a Royal visit on his behalf in Africa. On 6th February 1952, Her Royal Highness was proclaimed Queen while she lodged at Treetops Lodge in Kenya. The world's newspapers printed the headlines, "The King is Dead, Long Live The Queen!". It was then that Princess Elizabeth was styled Queen Elizabeth II. The young and beautiful Queen returned to London Airport less than a week after having left her father, The King, waving her goodbye from the runaway. She returned to the United Kingdom to be met by an entourage which included her uncle, The Duke of Gloucester, and the Prime Minister, Sir Winston Churchill. Over 65 years have passed since the death of her father, but The Queen continues to amaze us all. At 93 years of age, she still is working as hard as ever, breaking every possible record set forth by any British sovereign. She has worked tirelessly for her people, here at home and overseas, never once putting herself ahead of her duty. Her accomplishments are great and her contributions to mankind countless. It has been her life's work to take the tired, old pieces from Britain's once vast empire and create a multi-faceted and flourishing organisation of nations which exist to this day in a friendly and unified manner where brotherhood and common goals unite the fragments of what once was.

"I have in sincerity pledged myself to your service, as so many of you are pledged to mine. Throughout all my life and with all my heart, I shall strive to be worthy of your trust."

Her Majesty Queen Elizabeth II
Coronation Day Speech, 2nd June 1953

The Commonwealth and its imposing place in the world is a direct attribute to the selfless and duty inspired will of Her Majesty The Queen. Her life and her legacy will always be synonymous with the period known as the "Second Elizabethan Era", but more so by the hard work and statesmanship involved in the care of the 53 member states which form the "Commonwealth of Nations".

It is an organisation and an establishment within itself to which Her Majesty is head. A living, breathing and ever-changing body encompassing 53 of the world's countries and over 2.2 billion people who look to Her Majesty for clear direction, guidance and statesmanship. The Commonwealth of Nations has matured much like The Queen herself. She has grown from a young princess into a figure of wisdom, knowledge and strength, a pillar of stoic continuity and fine diplomatic ingenuity. Her Commonwealth has grown from the broken and fractured remnants of Empire to an institution to be recognised for its efforts, its relationships and its many different cultures which are united in diversity.

She has spent decades nurturing each relationship within the Commonwealth and it is due to her knowledge and diplomatic abilities that she was able to partake in her creation's 50th anniversary. Much like Her Majesty, the Commonwealth has seen decades of good and bad, but it is the example set forth and the gentle mothering by Her Majesty which has kept this extraordinary social project on par. This international milestone is not just the Commonwealth's 50th anniversary, but a celebration of delicate balance and steady guidance which it would not have had without its builder, The Queen. From the remnants of Empire, to a new era and brand of brotherhood, it has been Her Majesty who has been not just instrumental in the making of, but the life's blood of this worldwide collaboration of states and people.

Many a book has been written and published about this famed stateswoman, but on such a rare and special occasion as becoming the longest reigning monarch in British history, it is only fitting that a book as unique as the celebration itself be made. As the Head of State of 16 nations and the Leader of the Commonwealth of 53 nations, Her Majesty has made quite a mark on the world stage in her 65+ years as Queen. In times of both good and bad, it was Elizabeth II who celebrated with and comforted her people. She has been the beacon of hope and light in dark days as well as the beaming example of how we as individuals and as a society should be.

It is not for her legend that we celebrate on this occasion, it is for the person she is, and the unforgiving duty that she has carried out without complaint or great blemish for the past six plus decades. More than just a Queen, this daughter, sister, wife, mother, grandmother, aunt, and niece did not apply for the job she currently has, a job for life which she never asked for and a burden that would see most, aged and immobile at her spry age, is something that Her Majesty does not take lightly. She dedicated her whole life to our service in which she has served her people and her nations around the world in a manner that has brought renewed popularity to the institution of monarchy and renewed worldwide fame and respect to not only her kingdoms and realms but the Commonwealth too. Her face has changed over the years, but it is without doubt still the most recognised face on the planet.

To us, her face is symbolic of the life she has lived and continues to give to us, her people. Her lines show age, but with that age we are shown that she has lived, laughed and loved. They show a journey on which we have travelled together over time, on which we are always led safely back home. Her smile is just as warm and captivating now as it was when she was a child, despite the turbulent and trying times which have come to pass. As we look into the face of our noble Queen, there is always that extra special something there which tugs at our feelings and emotions, the sense of pride in her life and what she has meant to the great nations of hers around the globe.

For many of us, she is the only monarch we have ever known, a monarch who is breaking through every record set and tested by those who have come before. We live now in the time of Elizabeth, a time in which every day is making history. History has marked the long and successful reign of Her Majesty, just in the way that time has given us a thousand years of British kings and queens. Many Royal milestones have been marked by portraits, paintings, music, poetry and buildings, but the next step in Her Majesty's reign is being marked by the fifth portrait of her profile by the Royal Mint. A new portrait of her has been commissioned and approved, and is now gracing the new pound coins which have gone into circulation. In an unprecedented way of valuing history, Her Majesty's reign can physically be seen on the very coinage which Her Government strikes.

Her Majesty The Queen and HRH Prince William KG
Garter Day, Windsor Castle.
Photo: Thomas Mace-Archer-Mills.

Her Majesty's Diamond Jubilee Weekend: Concert at Buckingham Palace, June 2012.
Photo: Thomas Mace-Archer-Mills.

Five portraits over billions of coins have marked this extraordinary reign, to which we can recall the years leading from her Coronation, to this new historic celebration from which she will again step in front of her Great-Great Grandmother, Queen Victoria. It may be difficult to recollect or even imagine, but at one time Her Majesty was a princess without the pressures of the world on her shoulders. She was a newly-wed wife and in love with a changing world and its people. It was in a far away and exotic land that she had her title of Princess stripped away as she returned to her native country as Queen to just about one-third of the world's population. As the sun never set on the British Empire, it has not yet set on the face of this young and energetic woman who was thrust into the world of statesmanship at the tender and young age of 25. It was a solemn day when her father King George VI passed, a day on which she was truly and unmistakably bound for her entire life to not only her nation and its people, but the territories and realms over the seas that hailed her accession to the world's most famous throne. As she arrived home and disembarked the plane onto the tarmac at London Airport, this young gentle wife and mother in mourning held the poise of a formidable Queen as she was greeted by her first Prime Minister, Winston Churchill, and an entourage of statesmen. Who was to know that after this sad homecoming, the woman who left a Princess and returned a Queen would in fact come to span one of the longest and most successful reigns that our rain-soaked and windswept isles have ever seen.

As the months, weeks and days of the longest reign in British history have passed, so has the world and the nations in which Her Majesty has reigned over. During her reign, the majority of the world's population was born, for she has been the only Queen most of us have ever known our entire lives. She has been there with us during every major event that has happened in our lives and continues to be the one constant that we can always look to as a source of fairness, light and example as she herself is the culmination of unbiased love, strong values and tolerance. She has championed women's equality and gay rights, amongst fairness and tolerance for those from different religions and backgrounds. Her reign has spanned six Archbishops; six Popes; and 13 British, 12 Canadian, 14 Australian and 16 New Zealand Prime Ministers. A total of 13 Presidents of the United States have sat in office since she became Queen, as well as a further nine Prime Ministers from Jamaica, seven from Barbados, St. Lucia and Papua New Guinea, three from the Bahamas, eight from Grenada, 11 from the Solomon Islands, four from St. Vincent and the Grenadines, and Belize, 12 from Tuvalu, four from Antigua and Barbuda and three from St. Kitts and Nevis. Her Majesty has had over 160 Prime Ministers during her reign, 30 of which are Prime Ministers from former Commonwealth realms. Some of her realms and territories have sought true freedom in the form of independence from the Crown, whilst others still remain as entrusted to her as they were the day she became Queen. Some have sought independence to become a republic from a Crown realm, whilst restructuring their governments and political aspirations to return to the Crown on their own accord, under

HM The Queen and HRH Prince Philip Trooping the Colour.
Photo: Thomas Mace-Archer-Mills.

their own Constitution and on their own terms. Papua New Guinea is such an example of this as it is Her Majesty's only non-hereditary realm. This nation gained independence from Her Majesty's realm of Australia in 1975 and set out to create their own constitution and laws of governance, whilst inviting Her Majesty to become their Queen. The position of Head of State was a position to which she was delighted to accept on behalf of the people of Papua New Guinea.

Milestone after milestone has fallen to her longevity and the foreseeable future sees Her Majesty presiding over many more to come. Jubilees, births, deaths, weddings and divorces are just a small fraction of what her life has seen and what her reign has held. She has met the longevity of her great-great grandmother in more ways than one and Her Majesty continues to oversee the continuation of the House of Windsor, which is a cause for celebration within itself. Four generations in total, three of which exist to secure our throne for decades to come, is a solemn testament to her life's work and perpetual stewardship of our nation. The Queen, The Prince of Wales, The Duke of Cambridge and Prince George stand in the face of history, each making their mark on the world stage, to contribute to the betterment, success and safety of their people.

Continuity is the running theme of our Crown, whilst our sovereign is the living breathing commitment to public service which personifies the State in all its glory - securing stability and prestige amongst the nations of the world. Her Majesty's reign is cause for celebration, but the milestones passed, the historic one at present and the many to come, will collectively showcase the true reverence that we have not only for our sovereign, but our Crown, our country and our place within the wider scope of humanity. Remarkably, the matriarch of our nation and the pinnacle of our Royal Family reached another milestone when she turned 90 in April 2016, thus creating another reason for celebration. She is now the longest living sovereign in our history, and each day which passes will see her creating her own personal record as the longest reigning monarch in our history. Future birthdays, Royal births and other Royal milestones are yet to come, and are attainable for Her Majesty to witness with the good health she enjoys. For as long as we have our Queen and as long as we secure our Crown, there will always be a reason to celebrate who we are as people and as a culture. It is due to the culturally rich attributes of our Crown which have had the greatest impact on our identity as a nation, attributes which are missing from many of today's modern republics. We as people are blessed with a history and culture which has been collectively enhanced by the presence of our Crown. Throughout the longest reign in British history, nations have fallen as new ones have emerged, great celebrations as well as great tragedies have occurred, the state of the world once teetered on the brink of nuclear war, and the doomsday scenario of the millennium came and went. Great leaders in politics and religion have been born and others have died as the natural face of our planet has changed tremendously since 1952.

No matter what has happened in our lives, for better or for worse, the one true constant that has always been, is Her Majesty The Queen. In this year of great celebration, it is a true honour to say that we live in a new and modern Elizabethan era - a privilege to be able to say that we have lived during the time of Elizabeth II. Today, we raise a glass to our nation's Royal House and toast: "The Queen!"

Thomas Mace-Archer-Mills
Chairman and Founder
British Monarchist Society
www.bmsf.org.uk

Thomas Mace-Archer-Mills at Windsor Castle.

A Royal Mixology

Famed as much for their love of the drink as they are for their prosperous or tumultuous reigns, Britain's monarchs have always indulged in their favourite choices of ales, liquors, spirits and wines, and Her Majesty Queen Elizabeth II is no exception. No matter who may have reigned at any given time in the one-thousand-year Royal history of these great islands, it was the ancient monarchs who were most notable for enjoying meads, beers, ales and wines. As the story of alcohol evolved and flourished throughout the famous dynastic reigns this country has seen, it was the courts of King Henry II, King Henry VIII and King James I (VI of Scotland) which attained notable fame for the multiple, grand wine and ale cellars which would come to be a lavish symbol of the might, wealth and lasting legacies of their reigns.

Much like King Henry II, who cultivated his own grapes at Windsor Castle in the 1100s, our own "Sapphire Queen", Elizabeth II, has taken to the hobby and pastime of the great monarchs of old by cultivating her own variation of liquid grape refreshment for production into an English sparking wine. In 2011, Her Majesty created her own vineyard at Windsor Great Park by planting 16,700 vines of Chardonnay, Pinot Noir, and Pinot Meunier under the watchful eye of the Ranger of Windsor Great Park, HRH Prince Philip. The first batch of successful and mature grapes were harvested in 2013 and for several years, the grapes were fermented, blended and aged in the Royal cellars to produce 3,000 bottles of English bubbly to be readied for sale by late 2016.

Windsor Castle
Photo: Thomas Mace-Archer-Mills.

The Royal stock of The Queen's bubbly sold out extremely quickly, whilst the demand for Her Majesty's blend of English sparkling wine forced a second bottling to be released in the latter part of 2017. So great is the interest and demand for Her Majesty's blend, that production is set to rise above 20,000 bottles within the next six years.

Today's champagnes and sparkling wines are often associated with wealth and affluence, with an English variation having been served at the Royal wedding of Prince William and Catherine Middleton in 2011. Throughout history, ales and wines were staple beverages of the upper classes and the landed gentry, whilst the poorer classes endured lesser quality stouts and meads. Regardless of the quality of the beverage, the drink was enjoyed by the masses as much, if not more so, than they are today, due to the simple fact that the water in and around England's cities was rife with disease and foulness.

However, water was still able to be consumed through the use of wells, though it was not as tasty and was certainly not as preferred to its alcoholic alternative. In taking preventative health measures, whilst quenching their thirst at the same time, the people of medieval England, Georgian and even Victorian England were ever so merry when it came to the imbibing of alcoholic liquids. The overconsumption of alcohol was rampant not only amongst the peasant classes, but the aristocracy, which eventually lead to the downfall of many great men (as it still does to this day). Some even met their demise with open arms for the very beverage in which they were loved, nourished and ultimately consumed.

Hogarth's Beer Street and Gin Lane.

George Plantagenet, 1st Duke of Clarence, 1st Earl of Salisbury, and 1st Earl of Warwick, KG (Knight of the Garter) was the brother of Kings Edward IV and Richard III, who played an important role in the struggle between the rival members of the Lancaster and Plantagenet families during the infamous Wars of the Roses. Originally a member of the House of York, George abandoned his family in favour of the Lancastrians where he would commit treason by plotting against his brother Edward, before trying to seek forgiveness and regroup under his familial banner. However, his actions were too little, too late. In 1477, King Edward IV tried and convicted his brother George of treason. As George was of noble blood, the brother of The King, he was entitled to die by a method of his own choosing. Rather than beheading, he chose his love of the drink. At his request, George Plantagenet was privately executed at the Tower of London on 18th February 1478, drowned in a large vat of his favourite beverage, Malmsey wine. Once his death had been witnessed and it was certain that there was no life left in his body, the wine-soaked corpse of The King's brother was brought to Westminster Abbey for burial in the very same vat of wine which had claimed his life.

George Plantagenet, 1st Duke of Clarence.

The death of George Plantagenet by wine brings new meaning to the phrase "to love something to death"! King James I of England (VI of Scotland) was a well-known lover of the drink, so much so that the vaulted undercroft of the Banqueting House of the Palace of Whitehall was specifically designed as a drinking den for him, where he would entertain his friends and "favoured" male courtiers. In honour of the drink which was so prevalent in The King's life, poet Ben Jonson wrote the following dedication for the Banqueting House's undercroft in 1623:

Since Bacchus, thou art father
Of wines, to thee the rather
We dedicate this Cellar
Where now, thou art made Dweller

It was not just the massed population of England who enjoyed the drink, but also The King himself who directly enjoyed, influenced and expanded the art of spirit making. In 1638, King Charles I granted a Royal Charter to the Worshipful Company of Distillers, where the liverymen within the company were given the sole right to distil their spirits throughout the City of London and Westminster, whilst being allowed to further carry out their trade 21 miles beyond the city limits.

The formation of the Worshipful Company of Distillers improved not only the quality of gin and its image, but that of the various other spirits which were common to England at the time. The Worshipful Company of Distillers also improved the workings of the English agriculture sector as surplus corn and barley was able to be purchased and used by the newly created distillers. In the modern age of spirit making and distilling, the Worshipful  Company of Distillers no longer has the sole authority on spirit making, but concentrates on their trade, their history, and charity, much like the other 110 Livery Companies within the City of London. According to City archives, the Worshipful Company of Distillers ranks 69th in the order of precedence, where its members are from the drinks industry as well as those still involved in the distilling practice and business. The heraldic motto of the Worshipful Company of Distillers is: "Drop as Rain, Distil as Dew".

Rising in the order of precedence of City Livery Companies much like the head on a freshly pulled pint, the Worshipful Company of Vintners occupies the 11th most important spot on the city list of Livery Companies. It is known as one of the "Great Twelve Livery Companies" whose motto is "Vinum Exhilarat Animum: Wine Cheers the Spirit". King Edward III granted a Royal Warrant to the Worshipful Company of Vintners in 1364 and it is due directly to the issuance of this Royal status that the company created a monopoly over wines imported from Gascony in the southwest of France. King James I empowered the Company to continue its monopoly through the Royal Charter of 1611 which further benefited the Vintners as it guaranteed them the right to sell wine without a license, which allowed it to become the most powerful and influential company in the wine trade. Members of the Royal Family have had an affiliation with the Worshipful Company of Vintners, such as The Earl of Athlone who was Master of the Company from 1934-1935 and the then Duke of Gloucester was also Master from 1953-1954. Though many of the ancient rights provided by its Royal Charter have long since been removed, certain rights and privileges remain. One of the most historic rights which to this day include Her Majesty The Queen, is the exclusive involvement of the Company in the ancient ceremony of Swan Upping. Swan Upping is an annual ceremony which takes place on the River Thames. It is a tradition which was begun in the twelfth century but was formally recognised through Royal Charter by King Edward IV in 1482. The original purpose for the act of Swan Upping, according to Joseph Chitty in his work *A Treatise on the Game Laws and on Fisheries*, was so the monarch could establish "how much land he must have which shall have a mark or game of swans" which by law would forbid the ownership of swans by "yeoman and husbandmen, and other persons of little reputation".

Today, Swan Upping establishes a census of swans, where their health and fitness is checked. The census of swans is conducted through a process of placing a numbered ring around the swan's foot. It is within this ceremony that The Queen's Vintners and also members of the Worshipful Company of Dyers take to the river in their row boats, known as skiffs, marked by the banners of each respectful company. Swans caught by the Worshipful companies of Dyers and Vintners are identified as theirs by means of a second ring being placed on the other leg of each swan "upped". For the first time in her reign, Queen Elizabeth II attended Swan Upping in her capacity as "Seigneur of the Swans" on 20th July 2009. This occasion was the first time that a monarch had personally attended the ceremony for over two centuries.

The ancient origins, connections, persuasions and affiliations between our past monarchs and alcohol prove that the drink is a large component of our history which can no longer go unnoticed or unmentioned. In modern times, it has been the consumption of liquors and spirits that have been associated with not only the drinks and drinking habits of royalty, but right down to the culture of cocktail parties which took hold during the early part of the twentieth century. The inception and very notion of a cocktail party in favour of a full evening of suited entertainment in Royal and aristocratic households met strong opposition, but as times changed and social attitudes became more progressive, the flow of spirits and liquors seemed to informally pool at the bottom, to which society would dive into from the top rungs of the social ladder.

During the nineteenth century, in the grand and stately country homes and inner London palaces of the social elite, drinks were rigidly regulated by their position within the evening's entertainment, to which they were traditionally regimented to being served after dinner. After feasting on courses, taking the wine and closing with a pudding and dessert wine, those assembled would retire on a contented stomach to enjoy their host's liquid offerings, usually in gender-specified drawing rooms and libraries. The newly inhabited Buckingham Palace was no exception to the social expectations and placement of drinks within the wider scope of proper evening entertaining. Although there was a time and place for a nip of liquid rejuvenation, it is well known that those dwelling within the newly decorated corridors of this grand palace were not immune to the aromas and persuasions of specific spirits and liquors.

Queen Victoria's favourite drink was a mixture of claret and single malt whisky. Her Majesty was a small woman with a large thirst, which was often quenched several times throughout the day. Often in the modern age of distilling, we see many fine whiskies finished in claret casks which is a lasting impression of Queen Victoria's love of alcohol. Queen Victoria's eldest son and heir, King Edward VII, enjoyed iced champagne as his tipple of choice, whilst his son and heir, King George V, enjoyed his whisky so much that he granted a Royal Warrant on 1st January 1934 to Johnnie Walker & Sons Ltd to supply whisky to the Royal Household. Though The King was a lover of whisky, his history with it is quite interesting indeed.

Queen Victoria.

George V was less frivolous and more serious than his father Edward VII. He placed a much greater emphasis on his duties as King which required him to concentrate on Royal duties and official State entertaining. Such entertainments would of course include dinners with spirits, wines and other alcohols, but early on in his reign the clouds of war began to gather.

The onset of the First World War saw great concern over spirits by both the government and His Majesty The King. It was feared that the war effort and vital productions were being hampered by workers and soldiers imbibing a bit too much. The Chancellor of the Exchequer, David Lloyd George, was adamant that alcohol could cost Britain the war and set out on a quest to reduce the amount of alcohol available for consumption. In a statement to the Shipbuilding Employers' Federation in January 1915, the Chancellor stated that his nation was "fighting Germans, Austrians and drink, and as far as I can see the greatest of these foes is drink". He went on to campaign for others to join him in a pledge to not drink alcohol during the war, to keep morale and productivity high, to ensure a clear and decisive victory for Britain.

The following April saw His Majesty The King support the Chancellor's campaign. He promised that there would be no alcohol consumption within the Royal Household until the war came to an end and although many followed The King's lead, it was his own Prime Minister, Herbert Asquith, who refused to heed the advice given by his monarch and carried on with his delight of drink. As a heavy drinker, the Prime Minster was said to accuse David Lloyd George of going too far in respect of limiting the consumption of alcohol.

Despite the protests of his Prime Minister, King George went on to set an example for the nation. He prohibited alcohol from being served at his tables, at gatherings and State functions. Much to the dismay of his guests, varied drink substitutes were served during the war, such as sugared water, juices and tea. Hoping to do as much as he could to ensure that his efforts were seen as a serious contribution to the national campaign, The King was further convinced by the Chancellor that he should show an additional example of his commitment by physically locking the Royal wine cellars. This would be seen as a total abstention from alcohol which would serve as a positive example for the working class. Despite the efforts made by His Majesty, the working class continued to imbibe, but not at the rate previously

King George V slaying alcohol.

seen before the Chancellor's campaign. Queen Mary, consort to George V, also played her part during the Great War by insisting that there be food rationing at the Palace, even before the public were asked to partake.

The uncrowned and self-indulgent King Edward VIII was very different from his parents, King George V and Queen Mary. He was frivolous as The Prince of Wales, as well as later in life as The Duke of Windsor. He rather enjoyed anything alcoholic at any time as The Prince of Wales and further took to alcohol consumption to escape the reality of becoming King with the possibility of facing a long reign "without the woman he loved by his side". Loved by his family and adored by the public, The Prince of Wales was very much a charming and popular figure. However, he was very partial to a stiff drink and pretty women – the perfect combination for lavish and self-indulgent cocktail parties. Needing a "place of his own" which was not "office like", such as his accommodation at St. James' Palace, Edward went off in search of the perfect property and took a keen interest in Fort Belvedere, Surrey. The Prince was granted use of the property by his father King George V, but not before The King asked with a smile, "What could you possibly want that queer old place for? Those damn weekends, I suppose". It was well known even to The King that Prince Edward enjoyed the playboy lifestyle and that this property would provide him with the perfect backdrop to entertain his friends of society standing, pretty aristocratic women and their friends.

Fort Belvedere, Surrey.

Fort Belvedere is where a love story would unfold, that of Edward, The Prince of Wales, and an American divorcee, Wallis Simpson. As time progressed, with the cocktails constantly on pour, the Prince eventually had a suite of rooms created for Mrs Simpson, in which she would make the fort her home. Living with The Prince of Wales, Mrs Simpson and Edward would entertain on a weekly basis, nearly every weekend in fact, hosting cocktail and dancing parties for their friends, aristocrats, courtiers, American and British men of society and affairs, statesmen, soldiers and sailors. As the parties grew more frivolous and the prospects of damaging the position of her lover, who would be King, more likely, Mrs Simpson vacated the fort on 3rd December 1936, only a short week before King Edward VIII's abdication. Once the abdication crisis of 1936 began to fade, the newly created Duke of Windsor (King Edward VIII) lived luxuriously in Parisian exile with his Duchess. The pair threw fantastically lavish and celebrity-studded cocktail parties, which was all the rage amongst the upper classes of French society. Recalling his days spent at Fort Belvedere within his memoirs, The Duke would state that at Fort Belvedere he "created a home at the fort just as my father and grandfather had created one at Sandringham… here I spent some of the happiest days of my life."

Whilst The Duke partied his nights away in luxurious and selfish splendour across the English Channel, his dutiful brother, King George VI, enjoyed and admired whisky much like their father, King George V. The Queen Mother (Queen Elizabeth, consort to King George VI) enjoyed several different drinks, her favourite being a gin and Dubonnet. Dubonnet is a sweet wine-based aperitif which was created by Joseph Dubonnet in 1846 and is still popular to this day. It is a sumptuous blend of fortified wine, herbs and spices, including quinine, which is also found in the ever-faithful companion of gin: tonic. The fermentation process of Dubonnet is stopped by the addition of alcohol, something we have all come to appreciate.

In her earlier years as The Duchess of York, Queen Elizabeth The Queen Mother was photographed "fishing for champagne" at a garden party in aid of the Princess Elizabeth Hospital for Children in London. Queen Elizabeth The Queen Mother was a product of changing times when she met, dated and eventually married the then Duke of York. She had come to accept the relaxed social attitudes attached to leisure drinks and cocktail parties, often using spirits, liquors and mixed drinks as conversation, party favours and entertainment itself. As family events unfolded and The Duke and Duchess of York

found themselves as King and Queen of the United Kingdom and Northern Ireland, it was not just the people who would toast Their Majesties, but Their Majesties who would often at times toast the nation and those around them. The Queen Mother's niece, the Honourable Margaret Rhodes, who was also at one time her lady-in-waiting, has described some of Her Majesty's dinners at Birkhall Estate to be "uproarious" in content. At the end of a meal, Queen Elizabeth would hold her glass high and start a series of toasts with "hooray for... There was even more of 'Down with...'" with glasses almost disappearing beneath the table.

This example further continues to show that Her Majesty Queen Elizabeth The Queen Mother made a point to use spirits as both a token of serious affection and a show of cheeky playfulness when in public and more importantly in the privacy of her own home. As Queen consort to her husband King George VI, it was a Canadian distillery in 1939 that created Crown Royal to honour the State Visit of the popular Queen Elizabeth and King George VI to Canada in that same year.

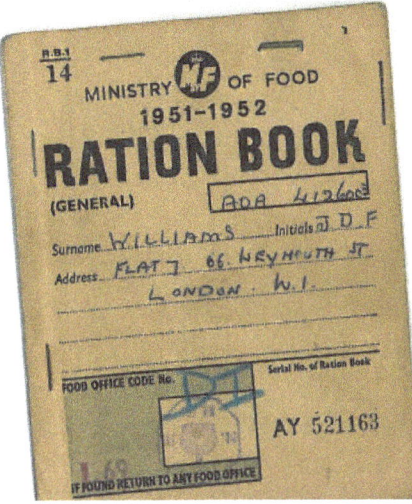

During the late 1930s and into the 1940s, war came to Europe, eventually engulfing Britain in conflict, which forced the nation to undergo strict rationing until the early 1950s. Official rationing commenced on 8th January 1940 with meat and staples such as butter, milk and sugar. Rations were distributed by weight, monetary value or points, and only obtainable through the ration coupon books provided by the government. However, luxuries such as alcohol (ales, beers, spirits and wines) and cigarettes were not officially rationed, but were limited and very expensive. It was a good idea to 'keep in' with the local grocer to whom one was registered for rationing, as the grocer would often reserve extras for favoured customers.

In 1952, two years before the end of war rationing, Princess Elizabeth became Queen Elizabeth II and began to progress with her own reign. It was at this time that The Queen Mother had a Royal Warrant issued to Gordon's of London to provide gin to her household at Clarence House, thus rendering Gordon's of London the only gin maker to hold two simultaneous Royal Warrants for two living Queens: one for Her Majesty Queen Elizabeth II, and the other to Her Majesty Elizabeth The Queen Mother.

Her Majesty Queen Elizabeth The Queen Mother enjoyed her gin, often mixing it with tonic or most famously with Dubonnet to create one of her most iconic pleasures in life, other than horse racing. Her love of gin and Dubonnet can best be summarised as she once noted before a trip, "I think that I will take two small bottles of Dubonnet and gin with me this morning, in case it is needed." Upon the death of Her Majesty Queen Elizabeth The Queen Mother, floral tributes including bottles of gin were left in memoriam of this famed Queen consort who was well-known to have loved her gin almost as much as she loved her people.

With the passing of the generation before, it is often the learned behaviour, tastes and likenesses which prevail in the present generation of power and knowledge. According to the Honourable Margaret Rhodes, Her Majesty Queen Elizabeth II's alcohol intake never varies. Following in her mother's footsteps, Her Majesty takes a gin and Dubonnet immediately before lunch. The Queen likes her drink to be served as one part gin and two parts Dubonnet, with two cubes of ice and a slice of lemon with the pips removed. She will then take wine with her lunch and further enjoy a dry Martini in the evening, followed by a glass of champagne before heading down for the night. In light of this calculated and timed consumption of daily alcohol, it can assuredly be said that Her Majesty continues to uphold the family tradition of a right "Royal" drink. According to National Health Service (NHS) guidelines, women should not consume more than two to three units of alcohol per day, which would be no more than a standard 175ml glass of wine (ABV 13%). Men should not intake more than three to four units per day, which would be the equivalent of a pint of strong beer, cider or lager.

In respect of such guidelines, one would most assuredly agree that Her Majesty likes to partake in the great British pastime of "knocking a few back". Despite what the NHS "recommends", Queen Elizabeth The Queen Mother owed her longevity (nearly 102 years of her life) to the positive attributes and healthy aspects of the many botanicals found within gin. Though drinking may be a part of the normal every day and informal way of life in this new twenty-first century, the old traditional ways of confining drinks to a set time and place through stiff, rigid and calculated servings of royal alcohol and its consumption, still reign supreme in the somewhat traditional rooms of Buckingham Palace, Windsor Castle, Sandringham House and Balmoral Castle.

As further confirmation of Her Majesty's fondness of a good, relaxing drink, it has often been cited in a well-known exchange over lunch between Queen Elizabeth II and her mother, the late Queen Elizabeth The Queen Mother, that Elizabeth II stated, "I wonder if I might have a second glass of wine?", to which her mother replied with a smile, "Is that wise? You know you have to reign all afternoon". Considering this uproarious exchange between mother and daughter, it is certain that even Her Majesty feels the pressures of her job, in which she too can relate to the work-related stress of her people. It is almost assured that these pressures and stresses associated with her position often lead Her Majesty to an extra, deregulated drink on some days of the week.

The Price of Wales not only adored his grandmother, but learned many of the royal rules of life from her experiences. He has also taken from The Queen Mother's lead on family traditions of alcohol consumption. HRH Prince Charles is said to enjoy a 50:50 Martini, which uses equal amounts of gin (a staple of his granny) and dry vermouth. Martini (suppliers of Martini vermouth) once caused a great deal of anguish to Her Majesty Queen Elizabeth The Queen Mother, when she had asked a butler to bring her a Martini and instead received a tall glass of warm vermouth. In The Queen's company during this trying time was the American journalist R. W. Apple. The Queen Mother looked at him and said, "Young man, I believe you're American from your accent. Do you know how to make a Martini cocktail?" "Yes, ma'am. I certainly do," he responded. The Queen Mother replied, "Please will you go to the pantry with the butler and instruct him how to do so." What was served to Her Majesty was the 11:1 Martini (proportion of gin to vermouth). She liked it so much that she kept asking for them all evening. In later life, The Queen Mother often carried a flask of gin in her handbag during the winter months. This was a small flask which she often asked her equerry to fill and place in her bag before leaving her home. She would explain, "I don't approve of heated cars. They are very bad for

your health. Many elderly people have caught pneumonia getting out of a heated car on to a freezing street. If one is cold when travelling, a nip of gin is a much more sensible idea."

Scotch whisky is undoubtedly The Prince of Wales' drink, with Inver House Distillers making a royal favoured Barrogill. This is a whisky which was specially chosen by The Prince after a private whisky tasting. His Royal Highness likes Laphroaig whisky, with the 15-year-old being of a particular preference. In his own right, The Prince of Wales issued a Royal Warrant to the Laphroaig Distillery in 1994, when he personally visited the distillery to bestow this great honour upon the company. His last visit to Laphroaig formed part of his 60th birthday celebrations in 2008. In 2015, Laphroaig celebrated 200 years of distilling.

Prince Charles' lovely wife, The Duchess of Cornwall, is considered a "special friend" of Laphroaig, which indicates a fondness of their products similar to her husband. In fact, Her Royal Highness is also known to follow in the footsteps of her husband's grandmother by enjoying a nip of gin from time to time. It is said that when she met with Prince William at St. James' Palace in 1998 to talk about her relationship with his father Prince Charles, Camilla emerged from the friendly meeting saying, "I need a gin and tonic". Gin and tonic seems to be a recurring favourite in the House of Windsor, so much so that amongst its tipplers we further include His Royal Highness Prince Edward, The Earl of Wessex and his father, Prince Philip. In his early days, Prince Philip took to gin and tonic to calm his nerves in the weeks and days leading up to his wedding to the then Princess Elizabeth.

Like his predecessors and their consorts, His Royal Highness Prince William, The Duke of Cambridge, and Her Royal Highness Catherine, The Duchess of Cambridge, will continue the tradition of royal association with spirits. Their preferences were already highlighted with their preferred drink of choice, the "Crack Baby Cocktail", which mixes fresh passion fruit with vodka and champagne, at their wedding reception in 2011. Prince William has enjoyed a string of alcoholic favourites over the years, such as Stella Artois and sambuca shots.

At the famed Mahiki nightclub in Mayfair, The Duke once enjoyed the famed "Treasure Chest" cocktail, which is made with brandy and peach liqueur, topped with a bottle of champagne and served in a wooden chest. At only £135, this cocktail is a bit steep in price for us mere commoners, but it is good to hear that The Duke of Cambridge can relate to us as he is said to now favour a more "affordable" pint of Guinness.

Catherine, The Duchess of Cambridge.
Photo: Thomas Mace-Archer-Mills.

The Duchess of Cambridge certainly likes something a little light and fruity and has been seen sipping on Mahiki's famed Pina Colada to bring her sweet enjoyment throughout the night. On less vivacious occasions, Her Royal Highness enjoys an association with whisky (much like monarchs of old) which she sips slowly.

Although His Royal Highness Prince Harry appears to favour anything coming across the bar, if the press coverage of yesteryears is anything to go by, it is not the case. Prince Harry favours premium vodka Cîroc Ultra, which is one of the few vodkas made using grapes. From time to time Prince Harry does like to pair a Red Bull with his vodka in favour of other mixers, such as sodas, tonics and the more nutritious fruit juices. I guess one serving of fruit (grapes) per glass is enough for the Prince, despite the recommended 4-5 servings per day he should be consuming. Although younger members of the Royal Family have taken to cocktails in very public places, such as nightclubs like Mahiki and other places

HRH The Princess Royal.
Photo: Thomas Mace-Archer-Mills.

owned by Prince Harry's friends, it is the older members of the Royal Family who still keep a stiff upper lip with a distinguished and dignified manner about them, when associating with the likes of alcohol. Though most of our Royal Family do like their favourite tipple(s), there are the rare few who do not partake in the imbibing of alcohol at all. The "Dry Windsors" include His Royal Highness Prince Andrew, The Duke of York who prefers a good old British cuppa and Her Royal Highness Princess Anne, The Princess Royal, who prefers a touch of fizzy (Coca-Cola) over the harder to swallow drinks of her siblings, Princes Charles and Edward.

Her Majesty has extended her interest in spirits by visiting several breweries and distilleries over her reign. She visited the Guinness brewhouse whilst on her first ever State Visit to the Republic of Ireland in May 2011. As she and Prince Philip toured the facility, a freshly-pulled pint was placed on the bar in front of her. She kindly smiled and stepped back whilst Prince Philip could be seen to want to indulge in the delight of a nice pint as he rocked back and forth toward the foaming drink, before finally backing slowly away. Though Prince Philip's favourite brew is known to be Boddingtons, one could see the smile on his face and the look of desire in his eye as the pint of Guinness sat lonely on the bar top.

As the fresh pint beckoned him like a child to a sweet shop, one can be assured that a younger member of the Windsor family would not have been able to just walk away without tasting the soft creamy foam on their lips.

The young and more modern members of our Royal Family are no exception when it comes to 'downing a few' in times of relaxation and/or celebration. As the younger generations of Windsors (both prince and princess alike) partake in the vibrant and colourful nightlife of the various clubs and pubs of our capital city, as well as the places in which they travel to and holiday in, we can always count on the drink as being a steadfast friend. The York sisters are casual drinkers; however, the excitement of the nightlife and the new experiences that come with a move across the pond call for a little more than casual liquid refreshment. In 2013, Princess Eugenie had taken New York City as her home and playground, and had been seen enjoying the nightlife and bar scene of the Big Apple time and time again. In between work, there was the occasional gala, courtside beers at the Knicks games, the occasional alfresco tipple, and late evening alcoholic excursions to the city's hottest night spots.

Princesses Beatrice and Eugenie of York.

As if one York Princess was not enough in New York, Her Royal Highness Princess Beatrice could not be seen to miss out on the action, as the two of them together posed a united front at a charity gala in Brooklyn. To celebrate her return to London in 2015, Princesses Eugenie and Beatrice were again soon out together, knocking back a few drinks, as they explored the haunts of their grandmother's kingdom. Other close relations throughout the years, such as Lord Frederick Windsor, have enjoyed the entertainment of cocktails and other associated recreational activities. Late evenings and early mornings of stumbling to the motor, or playing in a fountain, have been caught by the paparazzi, showing us just how friendly the drink is to our younger generation of Royals. But no harm, no foul, we all have enjoyed forgetting ourselves every now and again with our intoxicating friend. So there is no harm when young Royals, such as Prince Harry, have fun coming in to their own like the rest of us, sharing the same altering experience no matter our station in life.

No matter whether in public or private, at sea in a boat, on land in a train, in a palace or rustic Deeside cottage, the Royal Family each has their own distinct drink of choice. No matter the occasion, spirits are always at the forefront of any form of entertaining when associating with The Queen and her family. Family gatherings, such as Christmas at Sandringham, see a multitude of drinks being consumed amongst the Royal Family. Dry Martinis are the chosen Christmas Eve drinks for Her Majesty The Queen, Prince Philip and Prince Charles when at Sandringham, whilst gin and tonic is served in frigid abundance to the rest of the family. Christmas is a very intense time for new members of the Royal Family who are truly brought into the fold of a Royal holiday break at Sandringham.

Photo: Thomas Mace-Archer-Mills.

A home filled with multiple Royal Family members, pets, servants and all that comes with a Christmas holiday, must have been nerve-racking for Her Royal Highness The Duchess of Cambridge during her first Christmas at The Queen's private Norfolk estate, Sandringham House. In fact, in 2011, it was the first time in decades that Her Majesty had invited such a large gathering of Windsors to her Norfolk home. A total of 27 members of the family had been invited which meant that due to insufficient rooms, some of the family had to be accommodated in the servants' quarters. This fact alone would have most certainly been a cause to have a drink or three, whilst Her Majesty prepared her home for the arrival of her immediate and extended family, on this most historic of Christmas holidays.

Now that The Duchess of Cambridge has been in the Royal fold for several years and enjoys new digs with her own family at Anmer Hall (gifted by The Queen) on the Sandringham Estate, Catherine can relax a bit more knowing that at the end of the formal Christmas Day gathering with her in-laws and after the mandatory Christmas cocktails have been consumed, William, the children and herself will be able to make the short drive from Sandringham House to their modest country manor to enjoy a peaceful and relaxing night's sleep in their own home.

Anmer Hall, Sandringham Estate, Norfolk.

It is not just during family gatherings or during formal holidays, such as Christmas, that we see corks being popped and spirits being poured amongst the Royals. No. This activity is more highly concentrated during formal functions of State when Her Majesty The Queen is entertaining.

State entertaining and formal banquets always begin with toasts to Her Majesty and the visiting Head of State, followed by large quantities of delectable delights, each course being accompanied by a different blend of wine or spirit. Over 20,000 people are entertained annually at exceptional receptions and banquets in which The Queen offers the very best in alcoholic refreshment to her guests. This form of entertaining does not include the extra 30,000 invitees that are entertained by Her Majesty at a number of alcohol-free garden parties. In fact, Her Majesty has had approximately two million people to tea during her reign. In addition to the thousands of cups of tea, cakes and sandwiches which are consumed by the public, thousands of litres of spirits have been emptied during the reign of Her Majesty The Queen.

Cocktail receptions by the hundreds have been held over the last 63 years, in which thousands of bottles of champagnes, wines and ports have been served. Her Majesty does not solely enjoy distilled spirits, but appreciates and amasses large collections of fine wines, ports and champagnes which are amongst the best in the world. The cellars in the Palace themselves are over 300 years of age, some of which were original to Buckingham House, when owned by The Duke of Buckingham. The house was bought by King George III as a country home for his Queen, Charlotte of Mecklenburg-Strelitz, which then became the official residence of British sovereigns on the accession of Queen Victoria, who was the first occupant of a renovated and newly constructed Buckingham Palace. Totalling a staggering 25,000 bottles within Her Majesty's collection, the duty of keeping these bottles in the perfect environment is quite difficult, as there are seven large vault-like rooms that comprise the royal cellars of Buckingham Palace. Worth over £2 million, the numerous bottles that are kept in the ancient cellars of this most famous of Royal residences, are kept under the protective and watchful eye of the Yeoman of the Royal Cellars, and administered by the Clerk of the Royal Cellars.

An important role in the carrying out of important Royal events and banquets of State, the Clerk of the Royal Cellars is an appointed member of the Royal Household, albeit a part-time position. This important post does not call for just anyone to stand in, but is selected from the most experienced senior wine merchants of the kingdom. The Clerk's duties include advising on all varieties of wine, supervising the purchase and acquisition of selected bottles and the quantities and the maintenance of not only the wines, but the entire garrison of alcohol, including spirits. He will use his expertise in and his knowledge of fine wines to provide the best possible advice on wine pairings for important State banquets, formal entertaining and other events of State which may require the Clerk's professional counsel.

In 2007, Her Majesty The Queen hand-picked and requested that Mr Simon Berry take up the position as "The Clerk of the Royal Cellars". Mr Berry is currently the Managing Director and master wine extraordinaire of Britain's oldest wine merchants, Berry Bros. & Rudd which is located opposite St. James' Palace in the heart of London and has been a lively trading hub of fine wines since 1698. Following in the great traditions of our past monarchs, it is commonly believed that Berry Bros. & Rudd supplied wine to George III although the company has no actual record of this. It is, however, documented that the

BERRY BROS & RUDD
WINE & SPIRIT MERCHANTS

company supplied the Prince Regent and when he became George IV. They also supplied The Duke of Clarence and presumably also when he became William IV.

Berry Bros. & Rudd is not just a simple wine company, on a good street, with Royal connections, but a witness, steward and maker of history. The company's long list of direct involvement in historic events includes their own wines being lost on board the *Titanic*. The archives of Berry Bros. & Rudd contain a "carefully typed letter" to the company from the White Star Line dated 15th April 1912 to which the letter "addresses the loss of 69 cases of the firms' wines and spirits onboard the ship. No mention is made of the lives that were lost". The company has provided shelter for Napoleon III in the cellars beneath the storefront and the supplying of smugglers running alcohol during the days of Prohibition in America. This famed wine merchant is not just in the wine trade, but the production of one of the most famous brands of Scotch whisky in the world. In 1923, Berry Bros. & Rudd created Cutty Sark Scotch whisky, which became very popular very quickly and drove demand in both the Bahamas and in America. To this day, it is one of the company's most successful beverage products.

Paving their own way through history, Berry Bros. & Rudd was the first independent wine merchant to create temperature-controlled wine cellars for their inventory in 1967. Their cellars hold approximately 8.5 million bottles of company and customers' wine, worth millions of pounds, both of which are components that add to the credibility of this company to be the source for an appointed member of the Royal Household. The company enjoys a Royal Warrant from Her Majesty The Queen and also a Royal Warrant from His Royal Highness The Prince of Wales. Given the extensive history of Berry Bros. & Rudd, and the centuries of expertise contained within this extraordinary company, it is understood why Her Majesty appointed Mr Simon Berry as her Clerk of the Royal Cellars. His experience, know-how and care of such valued fermentation with his own company has given Her Majesty the confidence needed to entrust him with her own wine acquisitions and collection. Such valuable bottles stored in Her Majesty's wine cellar include a sherry dating from 1660 as well as "newer" wines such as Château Léoville Barton 1988, Château Chasse Spleen 1990, Château Batailley 1994, Château Latour à Pomerol 1995, Château Fonroque 1995, Château Beau-Site 1995, Nuits St. George 1996, as well as Château Meyney 1996, which are housed together with South African Chardonnays and New Zealand Sauvignon Blancs.

These rare and vintage wines give way to a variety of exclusive ports such as 1963 Fonseca and Quinta do Noval. It is not only the wine cellars at Buckingham Palace that hold such rarities and bottles of value, as it can be assumed that each of the residences that are inhabited by Her Majesty undoubtedly hold a plethora of such alcoholic treasures. No matter where The Queen may entertain, be it formal or informal, we can rest assured that nothing but the finest of alcohols is being served. Even whilst The Queen and Royal Family are "off duty" and away at Balmoral for their private summer holiday, the bottles still pop and the spirits flow like the River Dee.

It is not always in time of celebration or State occasioning that the drink is used in and around the Royal Family. It is often used in times of despair to relieve the stresses of public life, such as in the case of the late King Edward VIII during and after the abdication crisis. King George VI and Queen Elizabeth each calmed their nerves during the Blitz and after long walkabouts where they surveyed the damage not only to the City of London, but their own home and Palace left by the bombs of WWII. The Prime Minister Winston Churchill was known to always have a drink with his

cigar, and in Prime Minister Tony Blair's case, it was used to escape a less than entertaining annual visit to meet The Queen in Scotland during his time at 10 Downing Street. Mr Blair was able to keep his wits about him whilst visiting Her Majesty on the annual Balmoral weekend, where Her Majesty extends her hospitality to the current Prime Minister of the day and his wife each year, for a weekend of rustic retreat at her private castle. Not known for their love of the wilderness or their less than luxurious lifestyle, the Blairs found this annual weekend to be quite trying and not in line with their own personal expectations of grandeur, as not much has changed within Balmoral since the times of Queen Victoria and Prince Albert. The castle is a fine example of Scottish rustic decor at its height. When asked about his Balmoral getaway, Mr Blair stated in his autobiography: "Using the bathroom on the other side of the corridor was a singular act of courage, sneaking open the bedroom door, glancing right and left and then making for it at speed". This quote really illustrates

Balmoral Castle, Scotland.

his resentment for the lack of en-suite fixtures one would have whilst staying at the Ritz or newly-renovated Savoy. However, 'Tony' and his wife, Mrs Blair, were not at the Ritz, nor were they checked in at the Savoy, they were guests of Her Majesty at her private home, where one would be honoured just to be considered for this most coveted of invitations and delighted to make do with what was available at The Queen's private residence.

Coping with the less than luxurious surroundings, Mr Blair looked forward to the abundant drinks that he described as "rocket fuel" which helped him survive the weekend. These drinks helped him relax, to the point which he described as, "The burden and the head got lighter". Knowing the relationship between "just call me Tony" and Her Majesty, it is surely speculated that The Queen needed her drink just as much as the Blairs needed theirs on this most uncomfortable of annual visits. Thank the good Lord that for every occasion, good or bad, of ease or stress we can always turn to drink to celebrate a right royal celebration or dreaded encounter!

It is not just the Royal Family, visiting Prime Ministers or invited guests that enjoy the refreshing liquid hospitality of The Queen, but those that serve her and her family on a daily basis. Those working "downstairs" were the recipients of good alcohol at bargain prices, as the staff bar in the Palace gave the servants access to quality but cheaply priced drinks and cocktails. Due to the cutting of costs at the Palace, the staff bar was closed as part of a savings scheme by the Comptroller of the Royal Household. Though their bar was closed, servants on duty are given two miniatures of spirits or port when they are assigned to the lavish banquets and parties held at The Queen's residences. It has been known to be written into some contracts that servants could "finish up the dregs" of fine wines left by visiting VIPs so as not to "waste" such quality alcohol. It is acknowledged that some of those employed by the Royal Household were known to have a problem with drink, however Her Majesty had always been supportive and sympathetic.

In July 2013, Mr Phil Dampier of the *Express* reported that, "Several years ago one (servant) fell down the stairs at a glittering state banquet right in front of her. The Queen just stepped over him and said: "Would someone please come and pick him up!" At the 2004 Christmas party, two servants ended up in hospital, one with alcoholic poisoning and another with a suspected broken ankle after falling over.

The servants work long hours, so booze has often been seen as a way of coping. Though alcohol can be a way of celebrating, it can also be used as a coping mechanism for those under the weight of stress, depression and addiction. The overconsumption of drink can lead to alcoholism and other health issues. Whilst this book is not written to glorify the use of alcohol as a tool for celebration, it is designed to illustrate how alcohol has historically been a component of national and Royal celebrations and how it has defined British culture for the many centuries kings and queens have sat on our throne.

This is the part of the book where I am supposed to break for a moment before continuing to the history of each spirit, to give you (the reader) a responsible disclaimer about the adverse effects of alcohol consumption. However, due to the very nature of this book and the use of alcohol as a tool for my own celebrations, I will leave such Public Service Announcements to the NHS or whatever health agency is the leading authority on such issues within the country that you are reading this book in. I think it is now time for us to raise a glass and propose the Loyal Toast: "The Queen!"

Photo: Thomas Mace-Archer-Mills.

Windsor Castle - Garter Day
Photo: Thomas Mace-Archer-Mills.

*Lorenz Tullio Santonocito
Director and Master Mixologist
M Den and Restaurants.*

The Royal Line-Up

An Interactive Timeline of Royal Namesake Cocktails

Cocktails by Lorenz Tullio Santonocito

Examining the monarchs and their consorts over the centuries, it is acknowledged that each has enjoyed their own tipple, to which they have sometimes chartered and endorsed specialised brands, or have forsaken them entirely during times of economic and social turmoil. From the anecdotes, to the fun facts, to the documented history contained within this book where spirits and the Royal Family are explored, each sovereign has been represented and at times identified by their specific liking of, or contribution to, the advancement of a certain spirit. *The Royal Line-Up* contains specialised cocktails which are meant to represent the personality and identity of each monarch and their consort. Within the cocktails themselves, you will taste the identifying components of the ingredients best chosen to represent each individual and their contributions to not only this nation and the world, but the very essence of the spirits themselves.

Since the reign of Queen Victoria, the world has seen a level and rate of unprecedented growth and change never before witnessed in human history. Two World Wars, abdication, fire, divorces, deaths, the rise of global terrorism, technological advances, weddings, births and jubilees, have helped shape the actions and responses of the Royal House of Windsor over the years. However, what has remained constant is the calming and soothing effect of a good cocktail.

Lorenz Tullio Santonocito of M Den and Restaurants.

No matter what has troubled, excited or caused the House of Windsor to take to the drink, it can certainly be proven throughout history that the kings and queens of this nation have certainly influenced the distilling of, sale of and use of spirits throughout the past one thousand year history of this island.

Enjoy the liquid representation of the Royal line-up within the pages that follow. These sumptuous cocktails, created by master mixologist Lorenz Tullio Santonocito, of M Den Restaurants, are sure to inspire, relax and help you enjoy our Royal history with a bit of historial reflection and calming refreshment.

The House of Windsor
(1917 – present)

- 50 ml cognac
- 15 ml orange Curaçao
- 10 ml pear brandy, such as Poire Williams
- 5 ml lemon juice
- dried star anise seed, to garnish

Method: In a Martini shaker, which should be ever present throughout the reading of this book, combine the above listed ingredients into the ice-filled shaker.

Shake this blend gently until the mixture becomes icy cold. Strain this cocktail directly into a cut crystal coupé and garnish with a dried star anise seed.

The House of Windsor is the Royal House of the United Kingdom and fifteen additional Commonwealth realms. Created by His Majesty King George V, the dynasty is of German paternal descent and was originally a branch of the House of Saxe-Coburg and Gotha, which itself was derived from the House of Wettin.

The House of Saxe-Coburg and Gotha succeeded the House of Hanover as sovereigns of the British Empire following the death of Queen Victoria. King George V was of the House of Saxe-Coburg and Gotha but was also the first sovereign of the House of Windsor, therefore making him one king of two Royal Houses: the Royal Houses of Saxe-Coburg and Gotha, and Windsor. Since then, King George V has provided four British monarchs to date, including three kings, King George V, King Edward VII, King George VI, and our present Queen, Elizabeth II.

The name of our Royal House was changed from Saxe-Coburg and Gotha to Windsor in 1917 due to the heavy feeling of anti-German sentiment in the British Empire during the First World War. During the reign of the House of Windsor, major social changes have taken place within Britain and the world. The British Empire participated in the First and Second World Wars, ending up on the winning side; however, Britain lost its status as the world's superpower during decolonisation. Much of Ireland broke with the United Kingdom and the remnants of the Empire became the Commonwealth of Nations which Queen Elizabeth II has made her life's work.

Queen Elizabeth II is the current head of the House of Windsor and is monarch of sixteen independent and sovereign states. These nations are the United Kingdom, Canada, Australia, New Zealand, Jamaica, Barbados, the Bahamas, Grenada, Papua New Guinea, Solomon Islands, Tuvalu, Saint Lucia, Saint Vincent and the Grenadines, Belize, Antigua and Barbuda, and Saint Kitts and Nevis. As well as these separate monarchies, there are also three Crown dependencies, fourteen British Overseas Territories and two associated states of New Zealand.

Motto: Dieu et mon droit: "God and my right"

The Queen Victoria
(1819 – 1901)

- 50 ml rye whisky
- 20 ml apple liqueur
- 10 ml lemon juice
- 5 ml maraschino liqueur
- 1 egg white
- lime twist, to garnish

Method: In a clean Martini shaker, combine all of the aforementioned ingredients and shake vigorously until frothy.

Pour in a cut crystal Martini glass and garnish with a twist of lime.

Queen Victoria:

"We are not interested in the possibilities of defeat. They do not exist."

"The important thing is not what they think of me, but what I think of them."

Interesting Facts:

Victoria was Queen of the United Kingdom of Great Britain and Ireland (1837-1901) and Empress of India (1876-1901). She was born at Kensington Palace. Her reign came to be known as the "Victorian Era" and was the longest of any monarch in British history until that of her Majesty Queen Elizabeth II.

Victoria was the only child of Prince Edward, The Duke of Kent and Strathearn, the fourth son of King George III and Queen Charlotte. Both The Duke of Kent and King George III died in 1820, and Victoria was raised under the close supervision of her German-born mother, Princess Victoria of Saxe-Coburg-Saalfeld, The Duchess of Kent. Victoria inherited the throne at the age of 18, after her father's three elder brothers had all died, leaving no surviving legitimate children to assume the throne.

Queen Victoria was barely five feet tall. She proposed to her husband, Prince Albert, and not vice versa. The Queen was raised by a single mother, and later became a single mother herself. Victoria was the first known carrier of haemophilia, an affliction that would become known as the "Royal disease". At least six serious assassination attempts were made against Victoria during her reign, most of which while she was riding in a carriage. Queen Victoria was part and partial to a specific cocktail composed of malt whisky and claret wine.

Queen Victoria had nine children: Victoria, Princess Royal; Edward VII of the United Kingdom; Princess Alice; Alfred, Duke of Saxe-Coburg and Gotha; Princess Helena; Princess Louise; Prince Arthur, Duke of Connaught and Strathearn; Prince Leopold, Duke of Albany; and Princess Beatrice.

The Prince Albert
(1819 – 1861)

- 50 ml Amarula Cream liqueur
- 25 ml dark rum
- 50 ml mango puree
- 1 pinch cayenne pepper
- 4 drops ANGOSTURA® aromatic bitters

Method: Combine and shake all the above ingredients in our trusty shaker until well mixed.

Pour into a crystal rocks glass and finish with 4 drops of ANGOSTURA® aromatic bitters.

Interesting Facts:

In 1841 he became chairman of the Royal Commission, set up to promote the arts. He became a successful art collector, buying valuable and quality paintings.

Prince Albert studied music, art history, law and philosophy.

Interesting Facts:

Prince Albert married his first cousin, Queen Victoria of the United Kingdom, at the age of 20. His untimely death at age 42 deeply affected Her Majesty and The Queen's memory of him guided her for the next 40 years of her reign. At his urging, Queen Victoria abandoned her Whig partisanship in favour of political neutrality. Disputes with Prussia in 1856 and the United States in 1861 ended peacefully, at least in part because Prince Albert succeeded in rewording Foreign Office dispatches so that they could not be construed as hostile ultimatums.

Albert and Victoria had nine children: Victoria (1840–1901), The Princess Royal, who later married Frederick III of Prussia; Albert Edward (1841–1910), who later became King Edward VII; Alice (1843–1878), later The Grand Duchess of Hesse; Alfred (1844–1900), later The Duke of Edinburgh and The Duke of Saxe-Coburg-Gotha; Helena (1846–1923), later Princess Christian of Schleswig-Holstein; Louise (1848–1939), later The Duchess of Argyll; Arthur (1850–1942), later The Duke of Connaught; Leopold (1853–84), later The Duke of Albany; and Princess Beatrice (1857–1944), later Princess Henry of Battenberg.

The King Edward VII
(1841 – 1910)

- 25 ml blended whisky
- 5 ml Grand Marnier
- 10 ml hibiscus liqueur
- 2 drops ANGOSTURA® aromatic bitters
- champagne

Method: In a crystal champagne glass, mix the first four ingredients together with a gentle stir.

Top the glass with ice-cold champagne. No garnish required.

Interesting Facts:

Edward was King of Great Britain from 1901 to 1910, having been heir to Victoria for nearly 60 years. He is the second-longest serving Prince of Wales after HRH Prince Charles. Edward was the eldest son of Victoria and her Prince Consort, Albert. Edward briefly joined the army where a liaison with an actress caused a considerable scandal. Albert died two weeks after visiting Edward where he reprimanded him for his actions, which caused Queen Victoria to partly hold Edward responsible for the death of his father.

Whilst serving as The Prince of Wales, Edward became a leader of London society, spending his time eating, drinking, gambling, shooting, watching racing and sailing. In 1863, he married Princess Alexandra of Denmark and they had six children, five of whom survived to adulthood. Edward also had a series of long-term mistresses. As The King, Edward threw himself into his new role with energy and his reign restored sparkle to a monarchy that been rather gloomy since his father's death 40 years earlier. He helped pave the way for the Anglo-French Entente Cordiale of 1904 and was also the first British monarch to visit Russia. In 1902, he founded the Order of Merit to reward those who distinguished themselves in science, art or literature. King Edward enjoyed the refreshing luxury of iced champagne as a favourite tipple.

King Edward VII died on 6th May 1910 aged 68, Buckingham Palace. His burial took place at St George's Chapel, Windsor on 20th May 1910.

The Queen Alexandra
(1844 – 1925)

- 25 ml dry gin
- 25 ml Campari
- 50 ml raspberry liqueur
- splash rose lemonade
- fresh raspberries, to garnish

Method: Build the ingredients in a red wine bowl (large glass).

Top up with rose lemonade and garnish with fresh raspberries.

Interesting Facts:

Alexandra was Queen of the United Kingdom of Great Britain and Ireland and Empress of India as the wife of King-Emperor Edward VII. She was The Princess of Wales from 1863 to 1901 which is the longest that anyone has ever held that title. Alexandra became popular with the British public after arriving in Gravesend from Denmark in 1863. Sir Arthur Sullivan composed music for her arrival and the famed Poet Laureate Alfred, Lord Tennyson, wrote an ode in Alexandra's honour:

> *Sea King's daughter from over the sea, Alexandra!*
> *Saxon and Norman and Dane are we,*
> *But all of us Danes in our welcome of thee, Alexandra!*

Alexandra's style of dress and bearing were copied by fashion-conscious women and she was known for her extravagant use of pearls and bejewelled chokers. Her public duties were restricted to uncontroversial involvement in charitable work as was the custom. She greatly distrusted and disliked her nephew, German Emperor Wilhelm II, calling him "inwardly our enemy" in 1900. In 1910, history was made as Alexandra became the first Queen Consort to visit the British House of Commons during debate. Later that year, onwards from King Edward's death, Alexandra was styled "Queen Mother", being a dowager queen and the mother of the reigning monarch. She was styled Her Majesty Queen Alexandra. As dictated by custom, Alexandra did not attend her son's coronation in 1911 as it was not proper for a crowned queen to attend the coronation of another king or queen. As Queen Mother, she continued the public side of her life, devoting time to her charitable causes as she did when The Princess of Wales and Queen Consort of Edward VII.

Queen Alexandra was an elegant woman who retained her youthful appeared in her senior years, but during the war her age caught up with her and she started to wear veils and heavier makeup. Shes topped making trips oversea and suffered increasing ill health. Queen Alexandra died on 20th November 1925 at the age of 80 at Sandringham House, Norfolk after suffering a heart attack. Her burial took place 28th November 1925 at St George's Chapel, Windsor in an elaborate tomb next to her husband.

The King George V
(1865 – 1936)

- 50 ml blended whisky
- 10 ml rose water
- 5 ml white wine
- 1 drop ANGOSTURA® orange bitters
- orange twist, to garnish

Method: Stir the ingredients in a mixing glass and gently swizzle until well mixed.

Continue to pour the cocktail into a room temperature rocks glass and finish with an orange twist.

Interesting Facts:

King George V was born Prince George of Wales in 1865. Following the deaths of his elder brother, Prince Albert Victor, and his father, King Edward VII, he ascended to the throne in 1910, becoming King George V of the United Kingdom and his consort becoming Queen Mary. The coronation of King George V was held on 22nd June 1911 at Westminster Abbey.

In the Royal Navy, he journeyed across the world, visiting places throughout the British Empire. His naval career was very distinguished and honourable as he commanded Torpedo Boat 79, HMS *Thrush* and HMS *Melampus*. Together as The Duke and Duchess of York, George and Mary lived at York Cottage, a relatively small house in Sandringham, where they lived more like middle-class people than royalty. He preferred to live a quiet life and enjoyed stamp collecting and hunting. George and Mary had six children; five sons and one daughter. His children were said to be scared of him as he was quite strict. Given permission to access state documents and papers as the heir to Edward VII, George was well prepared for his role as a king. As a supportive wife who often helped him write speeches, George permitted Mary to access his papers.

King George V visited his soldiers more than 450 times during the First World War. He further made over 300 hospital visits to injured servicemen and was severely injured himself during the war when he was thrown from his horse in France. King George V is responsible for changing the name of the Royal Family to 'Windsor' in 1917. In 1920, King George V granted Johnnie Walker a Royal Warrant for their Scotch Whisky.

The Queen Mary
(1867 – 1953)

- 50 ml Aperol liqueur
- 10 ml lemon juice
- 10 ml liquid sugar
- 20 ml apple juice
- 1 egg white
- violet flower, to garnish

Method: With ice, combine and shake all the ingredients in our trusty Martini shaker until the blend is sufficiently chilled.

Double strain this cocktail into a tulip glass and garnish with a violet flower to finish.

Interesting Facts:

Queen Mary was the Queen consort of King George V of the United Kingdom, who was also Emperor of India. In 1891, Princess Mary, who was very much liked by Queen Victoria to be a Royal bride, became engaged to her double second cousin once removed, Prince Albert Victor, the eldest son of the future King Edward VII. However, with only a few weeks to go before the wedding, Prince Albert Victor died of influenza leaving Mary without a husband. Queen Victoria still favoured Mary and further arranged for her to marry Albert Victor's brother, Prince George, later King George V. They were married at St. James' Palace, London, on 6th July 1893.

Following the First World War, Queen Mary continued her public duties, and suffered personal tragedy when her youngest son, Prince John, expired at the age of 13. A year after his Silver Jubilee in which Queen Mary was instrumental on celebratory visits and events, King George V died. As a dowager queen, Mary continued her charitable duties into old age and supported the war effort during the Second World War. After suffering with lung cancer, Queen Mary died of the disease at Marlborough House on 24th March 1953.

The King Edward VIII
(1894- 1972)

- 25 ml dark rum
- 20 ml Campari
- 15 ml apricot liqueur
- 3 drops of chocolate bitter
- dehydrated apricot, to garnish

Method: In a mixing glass, stir all the ingredients and swizzle until well mixed.

Pour the cocktail into a crystal highball glass full of ice, and garnish with a dehydrated apricot.

Interesting Facts:

King Edward VIII is the only British sovereign to abdicate his throne voluntarily. He abandoned his duty and his people in 1936 to marry the American divorcee Wallis Simpson. Uncrowned, he was king for less than a year, making 1936 'The Year of The Three Kings'. Prince Edward was the eldest child of King George V and Queen Mary and was christened Edward Albert Christian George Andrew Patrick David, the last four names being patron saints of the countries of the British Isles. Privately, he was known to friends and family as David. He joined the Grenadier Guards in World War One and was not allowed to see active service at the front – something he had wanted to do. Throughout the 1920s, Edward undertook extensive foreign tours particularly within the empire, representing his father around the world, where he would also visit areas of high unemployment during the economic depression of the 1930s. Such tours made Prince Edward a very popular Royal figure.

As The Prince of Wales, Edward had affairs with several married women in the 1920s. He met Wallis Simpson, the wife of an American businessman, and fell madly in love with her. The two carried on their love affair against the wishes of King George V and Queen Mary. In January 1936, Edward became King and in October of the same year, Wallis Simpson was granted a divorce from her husband. When George V died, Edward flew to London from Sandringham, becoming our first monarch to take an aircraft. He was also the first British monarch with a pilot's licence, which he had gained around 1920. It became clear that the new king's intent was to marry her, against the advice of many of his advisors who did not believe that Edward, as head of the Church of England, should marry a divorced woman. All attempts to find a solution failed and so, on 10th December, Edward signed the instrument of his own abdication and went into exile in France. In June 1937, Edward married Wallis Simpson at their château and the couple were created The Duke and Duchess of Windsor. In 1937, before the onset of World War Two, The Duke and Duchess met with Adolf Hitler.

Soon after the outbreak of the war and due to apparent Nazi sympathies, The Duke was appointed governor of the Bahamas where he remained in the post until the end of the war, when he and The Duchess returned to France.

Throughout his life, The Duke seldom visited England and when he did, it was to attend the funerals of family members. The wounds of abdication never fully healed to which much bitterness between The Duke and his family remained. Edward, The Duke of Windsor, died of throat cancer on 28th May 1972 in Paris. He is buried at the Royal cemetery at Frogmore, far from his family, but alongside his love, Wallis Simpson.

The Wallis Simpson
(1896 – 1986)

- 60 ml bourbon whisky
- 5 ml maple syrup
- 2 dashes of ANGOSTURA® aromatic bitters
- orange twist, to garnish

Method: In a mixing glass, stir all the ingredients together and strain directly into a rocks glass over ice.

Garnish with an orange twist.

Interesting Facts:

The romance between Wallis Simpson and The Duke of Windsor caused one of the biggest scandals in the history of the British monarchy. Wallis was a twice-divorced American who captured the heart of Edward, The Prince of Wales. Their love affair would see him abdicate his throne and abandon 486 million of his subjects in order to marry her.

Simpson was born Bessie Wallis Warfield on 19th June 1896, in Blue Ridge Summit, Pennsylvania. Ironically, Bessie Wallis Warfield's genealogy gave her technically more English blood than members of the British Royal Family. Before her first divorce was finalised in late 1927, Wallis had already met the divorced, well-to-do Anglo-American businessman, Ernest Simpson. Together, Wallis and Ernest moved to Europe where he ran his family's shipping business from London, whilst she stayed with friends in the south of France. Soon after the move, Wallis accepted Ernest's proposal and married in July 1928. In London, the Simpsons fell into a circle of well-connected American expatriates, and became friendly with Thelma, Viscountess Furness, who, though married, was also the mistress of The Prince of Wales, heir to the British throne. Simpson was known for her scathing wit and clever banter as a dinner guest and captivated Prince Edward. Edward became a frequent dinner guest of Mr and Mrs Simpson.

Buckingham Palace courtiers became quite distressed by the affair of The King's eldest son with the married, once-divorced American woman. The Prince made no show of concealing his true feelings and was visually deeply in love with Wallis. When it was found out by Wallis that her husband was having an affair in New York, she hired a lawyer recommended by Prince Edward. Edward and Wallis were married on 3rd June 1937 and were styled The Duke and Duchess of Windsor by Edward's brother, King George VI. However, not one member of the Royal Family was present. The Anglican cleric who performed the wedding ceremony of The Duke and Duchess was formally reprimanded. After the wedding took place, The Duke received a letter from his brother, stating that any children resulting from his marriage to Wallis would not be of Royal standing and furthermore that his Duchess would not be entitled to the style of "Her Royal Highness (HRH)".

After returning from the Bahamas at the conclusion of World War Two, The Duchess of Windsor regularly appeared on lists of the world's best-dressed women. She and The Duke spent most of their days after the abdication in glamorous exile, throwing cocktail parties and dinners at their homes in Paris and the south of France.

The Duke died on 28th May 1972 and The Duchess was invited to stay at Buckingham Palace for his funeral. A few years after burying her husband, Wallis began to suffer increasing health problems, including coronary artery disease, and died at her home in Paris on 24th April 1986. The bulk of her estate was left to the Pasteur Institute, a leader at the time in HIV/AIDS research.

The King George VI
(1895 – 1952)

- 50 ml bourbon whisky
- 1 tsp fig marmalade
- 1 pinch fennel pollen
- 5 ml absinthe
- 10 ml dry sherry
- 4 drops balsamic vinegar
- dehydrated orange, to garnish

Method: In our well-used Martini shaker, add the ingredients to the shaker with two cubes of ice.

Shake the ingredients well until the ice has broken into small chips and strain the cocktail into a Martini glass. Garnish with a dehydrated orange.

Interesting Facts:

George VI was one of only five English (or Anglo-British) monarchs to succeed the throne in the lifetime of his predecessor. Born Albert "Bertie" Frederick Arthur George Saxe-Coburg-

Gotha on 14th December 1895 at Sandringham House in Norfolk, King George VI was the second son of The Duke of York, later George V. He was brother to King Edward VIII who abdicated his throne, whilst leaving the British monarchy in turmoil. King George was the third sovereign of the House of Windsor and was known to suffer from a stubborn stammer as conceptualised in the film *The King's Speech*. As King, he lacked the self-confidence needed to be an effective public speaker, but overcame such difficulties with the help of his wife and a speech therapist. The King would eventually become one of the most popular monarchs to date.

As a child, Bertie was often unwell. He suffered from having knock knees and was naturally left-handed. Both of these traits would be corrected through difficult and often, at times, uncomfortable methods. In 1909, George attended Dartmouth Naval College and went on to join the Royal Navy and, furthermore, the Royal Air Force. He saw action in World War One at the Battle of Jutland. In 1920, he was created The Duke of York and began to take on various Royal duties which led him to a chance encounter with Lady Elizabeth Bowes-Lyon, the youngest daughter of the 14th Earl of Strathmore. The two were finally married in 1923 after Elizabeth had turned down his proposal of marriage several times. Together, they had two daughters, Elizabeth and Margaret, which The King referred to his family as "we four". Following the abdication of his elder brother, Edward VIII, George was proclaimed King on 12th December 1936 ('The Year of The Three Kings) and crowned at Westminster Abbey in May the following year.

Shortly after the coronation, King George VI and Queen Elizabeth paid State Visits to France in 1938, and to Canada and the United States in 1939, making King George VI the first British monarch to visit America. During the World War Two, King George was a rallying point for his people and visited Allied armies on several battlefronts, where he would tour the home front extensively.

The King created the George Cross award for courage which recognised recipients with 'acts of the greatest heroism or of the most conspicuous courage in circumstances of extreme danger'. During the war, the Royal Family refused to leave Britain. They stood tall in the face of danger and undertook active involvement in the war effort which won them many admirers. Although his symbolic leadership was crucial to his subjects during World War Two, The King's reign was perhaps most important for the quick acceleration and evolution of the British Empire into the Commonwealth of Nations.

In the years after the war, The King's health deteriorated. After sending off his daughter, Princess Elizabeth, on a Commonwealth tour in February of 1952, His Majesty expired during his sleep on 6th February, a few months after undergoing an operation for lung cancer. His daughter subsequently became Queen.

The Queen Mother
(1900 – 2002)

- 50 ml gin
- rhubarb cordial
- rhubarb foam
- anise seed, to garnish
- dehydrated rhubarb, to garnish
- apple slice, to garnish

Method: In a mixing glass, stir the gin and rhubarb cordial together and double strain into a crystal wine swirl glass. Top with rhubarb foam and garnish with an anise seed, dehydrated rhubarb and an apple slice.

Interesting Facts:

Elizabeth Angela Marguerite Bowes-Lyon was born on 4th August 1900, at St. Paul's Walden Bury in Hertfordshire. She was the youngest daughter born to the 14th Earl of Strathmore and his wife. Elizabeth was privately educated, first by her mother and then by a series of governesses. Her happy and loving family childhood was interrupted by the outbreak of World War One, in which one of her brothers was killed. After the war, she became a much

sought-after débutante, and the most persistent of her suitors was the brother of her good friend, Princess Mary, the second son of King George V, the young Albert "Bertie", The Duke of York. Although she twice declined his proposals, they were married at Westminster Abbey on 26th April 1923. Exiting the Abbey, Elizabeth impulsively laid her bridal bouquet on the tomb of the Unknown Warrior, a gesture that led the British public to take her into their hearts for the rest of her life. This act has become a Royal tradition and is followed by Royal brides to this day.

Elizabeth was kind, caring and compassionate. She provided constant support and encouragement for her husband and would further make him more confident and sociable. Elizabeth provided him with the greatest happiness he had known and further contributed to the caring family unit their two daughters, Elizabeth and Margaret, would come to cherish. When The Duke of York became King George VI in December 1936, Elizabeth became Queen. The King was strengthened by the knowledge that he could rely on the support and comfort of his wife and the encouragement of his daughters. Queen Elizabeth was installed into the Order of the Garter shortly after the abdication crisis of 1936. Despite her sympathetic nature, she never forgave Edward VIII or Wallis Simpson for what she considered dereliction of duty. Elizabeth was convinced, and remained so until her death, that the burdens of kingship shortened her husband's life.

Upon the outbreak of World War Two in September 1939, The Queen's life and work took on added dimensions. When Buckingham Palace was bombed, she said, "I'm glad we've been bombed. It makes me feel I can look the East End in the face." She was determined to offer real resistance if the Germans invaded and practiced regularly firing a revolver. When asked why she and her daughters had not gone abroad for safety like many of the continental Royal families, she answered, "My daughters could not go without me, I could not go with The King, and The King will never go." Recognising the powerful symbolism of

The Queen, German dictator Adolf Hitler described her as the "most dangerous woman in Europe".

After the death of The King, Queen Elizabeth was styled 'Queen Elizabeth The Queen Mother' upon the accession of her daughter, Queen Elizabeth II. She pursued her own interests: buying and restoring the Castle of Mey in Scotland; farming; gardening; fishing; raising corgis; and horse racing. She also spent time with her grandchildren, and imbued in them a sense of royal responsibility and a fondness for outdoor pursuits. On 15th July 1980, the Archbishop of Canterbury said at the 80th birthday commemorative service of The Queen Mother that she was "the human face of Royalty". Queen Elizabeth is a beloved Royal figure best known for her sprightly zest for life, a famous aura of gin and tonics, horse racing and camp humour.

The Castle of Mey.

The Queen Elizabeth II
(1926 – present)

- 40 ml gin
- 5 ml lemon juice
- 10 ml violet liqueur
- 10 ml hibiscus liqueur
- 20 ml Earl Grey tea
- violet flower, to garnish

Method: In our well-used Martini shaker, combine the aforementioned ingredients into the ice-filled shaker.

Make sure to shake this blend vigorously until frothy cold. Double strain into a Martini glass and garnish with a violet flower.

Interesting Facts:

Queen Elizabeth II is undoubtedly the most famous and most photographed woman in the world. She is our longest living, longest serving and longest reigning monarch. Elizabeth II is the first monarch in our nation's history to celebrate a Blue Sapphire Jubilee and is the first Head of State to open is

HM Queen Elizabeth II by Georgina Barclay.

the first British monarch to be formally versed in mechanics and to be trained on how to change a spark plug. two Olympic games in two different countries. Born in 1926, Elizabeth Alexandra Mary is the first British monarch to be formally versed in mechanics and to be trained on how to change a spark plug.

Queen of 16 realms, 14 British Overseas Territories and the Head of the Commonwealth of Nations of 53 individual countries. Queen Elizabeth II is a walking history book. The first British monarch to address a joint meeting of the United States Congress, Elizabeth was born in London as the eldest child of The Duke and Duchess of York, later King George VI and Queen Elizabeth. She began to undertake public duties during the Second World War, serving in the Auxiliary Territorial Service, and became Colonel of the Grenadier Guards on her 15th birthday. In 1947, she married Philip, The Duke of Edinburgh, a former prince of Greece and Denmark, with whom she has four children: Charles, The Prince of Wales; Anne, The Princess Royal; Prince Andrew, The Duke of York; and Prince Edward, The Earl of Wessex.

For the 2012 London Olympics, Her Majesty played herself in a short film titled *Happy and Glorious* as part of the opening ceremony, alongside Daniel Craig as James Bond. On 4th April 2013, The Queen received an honorary BAFTA for her patronage of the film industry. She was called "the most memorable Bond girl yet" at the awards ceremony. The Queen surpassed her great-great-grandmother, Queen Victoria, to become the longest-lived British monarch in December 2007, and the longest reigning British sovereign on 9th September 2015. She is the longest reigning Queen regnant in history and the world's oldest reigning monarch. Her Majesty became the longest serving current Head of State following the death of King Bhumibol of Thailand on 13th October 2016.

HRH Prince Philip. Portrait by Paliano.

The Prince Philip
(1921 - present)

- 50 ml Boddingtons beer
- 20 ml Campari
- 10 ml lime juice
- bitter lemonade

Method: Build the cocktail in a highball glass over ice, then top with bitter lemonade.

No garnish is needed.

Interesting Facts:

Prince Philip, The Duke of Edinburgh, is the consort of Queen Elizabeth II. He only retired from public duties in August 2017 at the age of 96. He will continue to support Her Majesty The Queen in a private capacity after sixty plus years of public service. Born in Greece, Philip was born into the Greek and Danish royal families. After Philip and the Greek Royal Family were exiled, Philip was educated in France, Germany, and the United Kingdom, where at age 18 he joined the Royal Navy. From July 1939, he began corresponding with the 13-year-old Princess Elizabeth (his third cousin through Queen Victoria of the United Kingdom and second cousin once removed through King Christian IX of Denmark), whom he had first met at a military function at the Royal Naval College, Dartmouth in 1934. During the Second World War, Philip served with the Mediterranean and Pacific fleets.

After the war, Philip was granted permission by King George VI to marry Elizabeth. However, before the official announcement of their engagement could occur, he abandoned his Greek and Danish royal titles to become a naturalised British subject. In doing so, Philip adopted the surname Mountbatten from his maternal grandparents at the suggestion of his Uncle Lord "Dickie" Mountbatten, The Earl of Burma. After a five-month engagement, Princess Elizabeth and Philip married at Westminster Abbey in November 1947. Just before the wedding, Philip was created The Duke of Edinburgh and upon his marriage to Princess Elizabeth, she became The Duchess of Edinburgh. Philip, The Duke of Edinburgh, left active military service when Elizabeth became Queen in 1952. With aspirations of a long naval career, Philip reached the rank of Commander before giving up his love of the sea to undertake official Royal duties alongside his Queen. The Duke of Edinburgh was formally made a Prince of the United Kingdom in 1957.

In addition to the four children he fathered with Queen Elizabeth II, Prince Philip has eight grandchildren and seven great-grandchildren, as of the end of 2018. Through a British

Order in Council issued in 1960, the descendants of Philip and Elizabeth not bearing royal styles and titles can use the surname Mountbatten-Windsor, which has also been used by some members of the Royal Family who do hold titles, such as Prince Charles, The Prince of Wales and Princess Anne, The Princess Royal. A keen sports enthusiast, Prince Philip has personally helped develop the equestrian event of carriage driving, an event which he still partakes in now in his nineties. He is a patron, president and member of over 780 organisations and serves as the chairman of The Duke of Edinburgh's Award scheme. He is the longest serving consort of a reigning British monarch and the oldest ever male member of the British Royal Family. He is also the longest lived male descendant of Queen Victoria, having surpassed (on 13th December 2016) Count Carl Johan Bernadotte of Wisborg (The Duke of Connaught's grandson) who lived to be 95 years, 6 months and 5 days old.

*HRH Prince Charles
The Duke of Rothesay,
Colonel-in-Chief of the
Black Watch.
Portrait: Georgina Barclay.*

The Prince Charles
(1948 – present)

- 40 ml vodka
- 20 ml Earl Grey tea
- 10 ml apple liqueur
- 5 ml lemon juice
- 10 ml Campari
- dried orange slice, to garnish
- violet flower, to garnish

Method: In our ever-ready and faithful Martini shaker, combine the aforementioned ingredients into the ice-filled shaker. Make sure to shake this blend vigorously until frothy cold with chips of ice in the mixture.

Strain directly into a white wine glass and garnish with a dried slice of orange and a violet flower.

Interesting Facts:

The Prince of Wales, Charles Philip Arthur George, was born at Buckingham Palace on 14th November 1948 and will be the fifth sovereign of the House of Windsor. He is the eldest child of Prince Philip, The Duke of Edinburgh, and Queen Elizabeth II, as well as heir apparent to Her Majesty The Queen. Known in the counties of the south-west of England as The Duke of Cornwall and in Scotland as The Duke of Rothesay, Charles is the longest serving heir apparent in British history, having held the position since 1952. The Prince of Wales is also the oldest person to be next in line to the throne since Sophia of Hanover (the heir presumptive to Queen Anne), who died in 1714 at the age of 83. Cambridge educated, Charles served in the Royal Navy and the Royal Air Force where on 8th March 1971, he flew himself to the Royal Air Force College Cranwell to train as a jet pilot. Following the passing out parade that September, he embarked on a naval career, enrolling in a six-week course at the Royal Naval College Dartmouth and then serving on the guided missile destroyer HMS *Norfolk* (1971-1972) and the frigates HMS *Minerva* (1972-1973) and HMS *Jupiter* (1974). He also qualified as a helicopter pilot at RNAS Yeovilton in 1974, just prior to joining 845 Naval Air Squadron, which operated from HMS *Hermes*.

In 1981, he married Lady Diana Spencer and they had two sons: Prince William (born 1982), later to become The Duke of Cambridge, and Prince Harry (born 1984), who became The Duke of Sussex. In 1996, the couple divorced. In 2005, Prince Charles married Camilla Parker Bowles in a civil ceremony at Windsor's Guildhall, followed by a blessing and luncheon at Windsor Castle. Charles' interests are across a large spectrum of humanitarian and social issues. His first love and relaxation method is the painting of landscapes.

He founded The Prince's Trust in 1976, sponsors The Prince's Charities, and is patron of numerous other charitable and arts organisations. Charles has long championed organic farming for which he established the Duchy Home Farm, run by the Duchy of Cornwall, which produces ingredients for the Duchy Originals Brand which he founded in 1990.

Charles has sought to raise world awareness of the dangers facing the natural environment, such as climate change and has helped pen a Ladybird book on this subject. As an environmentalist, he has received numerous awards and recognition from environmental groups around the world. The Prince has been outspoken on the role of architecture in society and the conservation of historic buildings, having played a large role in the development of the old Chelsea Barracks complex in central London. Subsequently, Charles created Poundbury, an experimental new town based on his theories, in Dorset in 1993 and has further created a similar village in Dumfries, Scotland.

Dumfries House.

HRH Camilla, The Duchess of Cornwall.
Photo: Thomas J Mace-Archer-Mills.

The Duchess of Cornwall
(1947 – present)

- 40 ml gin
- 10 ml chablis syrup
- 1 tsp orange blossom honey
- 5 ml lemon juice
- 5 ml lapsang souchong tea

Method: In that trusted Martini shaker, which should not be far from you at this point in time, combine the above listed ingredients into the ice-filled shaker.

Shake this blend lightly until the mixture becomes somewhat froid.

Double strain this cocktail directly into an orange-flavoured sugar-rimmed Martini glass. No garnish is necessary.

Interesting Facts:

Camilla, The Duchess of Cornwall (née Camilla Rosemary Shand), previously Parker Bowles, was born 17th July 1947 to Major Bruce Shand and the Honourable Rosalind Cubitt, the daughter of Roland Cubitt, 3rd Baron Ashcombe. Camilla is the second wife of Prince Charles, The Prince of Wales. Out of respect for Prince Charles' first wife, Diana, The Princess of Wales, Camilla uses the title The Duchess of Cornwall, which is her husband's secondary designation. In Scotland, she is known as The Duchess of Rothesay. Reared in East Sussex and South Kensington, Camilla was educated in England, Switzerland and France. In 1973, Camilla married British Army officer Andrew Parker Bowles, with whom she has two children, Tom and Laura. The couple divorced in 1995.

Before and after the first marriages of both Camilla and Charles, the two engaged in a relationship for many years, for which their love was true and lasting. Their ongoing relationship outside of wedlock became highly publicised in the media throughout the 1990s and attracted worldwide scrutiny from several different outlets. Despite infidelity on the part of their spouses, the world's media remained quite keen to create a story based solely on the actions of Charles and Camilla. In 2005, true love triumphed after years of upset and discord to flourish into a civil marriage ceremony at Windsor's Guildhall, which was followed by a blessing ceremony by The Archbishop of Canterbury at St George's Chapel, Windsor Castle. The blessing was attended by Her Majesty The Queen, Princes Philip, and Princes William and Harry, as well as many other members of the Royal Family. As HRH The Duchess of Cornwall, Camilla assists The Prince of Wales with his official duties. She is also a patron, president and a member of numerous charities and organisations. Since 1994 and before entering into Royal life, Camilla has taken action on osteoporosis, which has earned her numerous honours and awards. She has also raised awareness in areas including rape and sexual abuse, literacy and poverty, for which she has been praised. Camilla has found favour as a member of the Royal Family, being made a Dame Grand Cross of the Royal Victorian Order and also a Privy Councillor by Her Majesty The Queen.

The Prince William, Duke of Cambridge
(1982 – present)

- 20 ml Scotch whisky
- 100 ml champagne
- 1 cube brown sugar
- 2 dashes ANGOSTURA® aromatic bitters
- sprayed with rose water
- orange twist, to garnish

Method: In a champagne flute, place a brown sugar cube in the bottom of the glass. Add in the ANGOSTURA® aromatic bitters, whisky and top off with champagne. Garnish with an orange twist.

Interesting Facts:

His Royal Highness Prince William Arthur Philip Louis, better known as Prince William, Duke of Cambridge, KG, KT, PC, ADC(P), is the eldest son of Charles, Prince of Wales and the late Diana, Princess of Wales. He is second in the line of succession to the throne after his father. Born in the Lindo Wing of St. Mary's Hospital, London on 21st June 1982, William was baptised on 4th August by the Archbishop of Canterbury in the Music Room of Buckingham Palace, on the 82nd Birthday of his great-grandmother, Queen Elizabeth The Queen Mother.

Prince William was affectionately called "Wombat" by his parents and later "Wills" by the press which has become a lingering nickname.

On 3rd June 1991, William was admitted to hospital after accidentally being hit on the side of the forehead by a fellow student wielding a golf club. He suffered a depressed fracture of the skull but did not lose consciousness. William was operated on at The Great Ormand Street Hospital for Children, leaving a permanent scar. During a 2009 interview, Prince William dubbed his scar the "Harry Potter" scar: "I call it that because it glows sometimes, and some people notice it—other times they don't notice it at all". Prince William was educated at four different schools within the United Kingdom and obtained a degree from the University at St. Andrews. He spent parts of his gap year in Chile, Brazil and Africa. He also took part in several British Army training exercises in Belize.

In December 2006, he completed 44 weeks of training as an officer cadet and was commissioned in the Blues and Royals. Two years later, William qualified as a pilot at the Royal Air Force College Cranwell whilst undergoing helicopter flying training to become a full-time pilot with the Royal Air Force Search and Rescue Force in 2009. His service with the British Armed Forces ended in September 2013 and it was announced in 2014 that William would take on a full-time role as a pilot with the East Anglian Air Ambulance service based in Cambridge. Though the position was a paid job, he donated his entire salary to the Air Ambulance Charity. Prince William left his position with East Anglian Air Ambulance in July 2017 to assume a more active role in Royal duties.

On 29th April 2011, Prince William married Miss Catherine Middleton at Westminster Abbey, London. Before the wedding, Her Majesty The Queen, created him the Duke of Cambridge, Earl of Strathearn and Baron Carrickfergus. The Duke and Duchess of Cambridge have three children, Princes George and Louis, and Princess Charlotte.

The Duchess of Cambridge
(1982 – present)

- 50 ml bourbon whisky
- 25 ml Earl Grey, pimento & hazelnut syrup

Method: Stir all the ingredients in a mixing glass and stain into a tea pot. Smoke at the end with cherry wood and pour into a tea cup. Enjoy on a nice cool English day. No garnish is required.

Interesting Facts:

Catherine, Duchess of Cambridge was born Catherine Elizabeth Middleton on 9th January 1982. She grew up in Berkshire, England and studied art history at the University of St. Andrews, Scotland, where she met Prince William in 2001 whilst both students in residence at St. Salvator's Hall. The two began dating in 2003.

Catherine is the eldest of three children (her siblings are Pippa and James) born to Michael and Carole Middleton, who in 1987 founded their family business, Party Pieces and now have an estimated worth of over £30 million. Catherine's father has ties to the aristocracy and has benefited from trust funds which had been established over 100 years ago. Her relatives have been reported to play host to Royals since 1929. During October 2005, Catherine complained about the constant harassment of the media through her legal representative, and in 2010 pursued an invasion of privacy claim against two news agencies and photographer Niraj Tanna, who took photographs of her over Christmas 2009. Catherine obtained a public apology, £5,000 in damages, and was further awarded legal costs.

In November 2006, Catherine accepted a position as an accessory buyer with the clothing chain Jigsaw, carrying out a part-time position until November 2007. Around the time of her 25th birthday in 2007 media attention surrounding her increased dramatically, prompting warnings from both the Prince of Wales and Prince William and from Middleton's lawyers, who threatened legal action. She simultaneously worked at the family party planning business in her role as catalogue design and production, marketing and photography until January 2011. HRH Prince William and Miss Catherine Middleton became engaged in October 2010 in Kenya whilst on a 10-day trip to celebrate Prince William passing his RAF helicopter search and rescue course. Prince William gave Catherine the engagement ring of his mother, Diana, Princess of Wales.

Upon her marriage in 2011, Catherine Middleton became known as Her Royal Highness, The Duchess of Cambridge, Countess of Strathearn and Lady Carrickfergus. In October following the wedding, Commonwealth leaders pledged that they would with the approval of their governments implement changes in the British Royal succession law to adopt absolute primogeniture which would allow for the first child of the Duke and Duchess to be next in line to the throne after their father, regardless of the child's sex.

The Duchess' impact on British and American fashion has been dubbed the "Kate Middleton effect" by the media. In 2012 and 2013, she was selected as one of the "100 Most Influential People in the World" by *Time Magazine*.

The Prince Harry, Duke of Sussex
(1984- present)

- 20 ml Grand Marnier
- 25 ml Kings Ginger liqueur
- 10 ml amaretto
- 10 ml lemon Juice
- 10 ml Campari
- 80 ml champagne

Method: In a large wine glass, simply build the cocktail in the glass and give a gentle swirl to mix the ingredients. Top with champagne and garnish with a dehydrated orange.

Interesting Facts:

His Royal Highness Prince Henry Charles Albert David KCVO, or simply Prince Harry as he is known, was born on 15th September 1984. Like his elder brother William, Harry was born in the Lindo wing of St. Mary's Hospital, London. He is the younger son of Charles, Prince of Wales and Diana, Princess of Wales.

Harry's mother, Diana, Princess of Wales wanted Harry and his brother to have a broader range of experiences than previous royal children. She took them to very different places that ranged from McDonald's and Disney World to homeless shelters and AIDS clinics. In

1996, Harry's parents divorced and a year later in 1997, Diana was the unfortunate victim of a terrible automobile accident which claimed her life.

Like his father and brother, Harry was educated at a series of independent schools and after passing the entrance exams, was admitted to Eton College across the river from his grandmother's residence, Windsor Castle. In June 2003, Harry completed his education at Eton with two A Levels. He achieved an overall grade B in his studies and excelled in sports, particularly polo and rugby. During his gap year, Harry spent time in Australia working on a cattle station like his father did and further participated in the Young England vs Young Australia Polo test match. He went to visit Lesotho where he worked with orphaned children and further produced the documentary, *The Forgotten Kingdom*. Since then, Prince Harry has created the Sentebale charity for the children of Lesotho.

Returning from his gap year, Harry chose a military career and underwent officer training at the Royal Military Academy Sandhurst where he was commissioned as a cornet into the Blues and Royals. He served temporarily alongside his brother and completed his training as a troop leader. In 2007–08, Prince Harry saw combat action in Helmand, Afghanistan where he served for over 10 weeks and served another 20-week deployment in 2012-2013 with the Army Air Corp. He left the army in June 2015. Harry launched the Invictus Games in 2014, and remains patron of its Foundation as well as giving patronage to several other charities, many of which are military related.

Carrying on in the footsteps of his mother, Harry has continued to raise the awareness of HIV and HIV testing. He took an HIV test live on the Royal Family Facebook page on 14th July 2016 and on World Aids Day, he teamed up with international superstar Rihanna who helped publicise HIV testing by taking the test themselves.

Prince Harry married American actress and divorcee, Ms. Rachel Meghan Markle on 19th May 2018 at St. George's Chapel, Windsor Castle.

The Markle Sparkle, The Duchess of Sussex
(Also known as the "American Princess")
(1981 – present)

- 50 ml vodka
- 25 ml Pimm's Reduction
- 20 ml lemon juice
- 50 ml strawberry & basil gin
- seasonal berries, to garnish

Method: Let's make this drink sexy and electrifying! In a vibrant looking Martini shaker, mix the ingredients above with ice and shake what your "momma" gave ya! Double strain this smooth mixture into a highball glass and top up with soda water.

Garnish this refreshing cocktail with fresh seasonal berries. If you happen to have a sparkler or table cannon, feel free to light it up and enjoy the sparkle of America's contribution to the British Royal Family!

Interesting Facts:

Rachel Meghan Markle was born on 4th August 1981. Reared in Los Angeles, California, Meghan graduated from Northwestern University with a degree in both theatre and international studies in 2003. During the years from 2003 to 2011, Meghan appeared on several small American television series whilst becoming a spokesperson and activist for several different charities and causes. From 2011 to 2018, Meghan was cast as the character Rachel Zane on the popular legal drama *Suits*.

In 2016, Meghan became romantically involved with Prince Harry. Meghan was introduced to Prince Harry by a mutual friend who had suggested a meeting and organised a blind date – it was love at first sight. Despite the modern times in which we live and the fact that Ms. Markle is bi-racial as well as divorced, Buckingham Palace was forced to issue an official statement in the wake of torrents of abuse and harassment which was directed at Meghan. The statement included support for Ms. Markle against such smears of racism, sexism and defamatory stories.

During a September 2017 interview, Meghan spoke in public for the first time about her love for Prince Harry, stating: "We're two people who are really happy and in love. We were very quietly dating for about six months before it became news, and I was working during that whole time, and the only thing that changed was people's perception." Later that month, they made their first public appearance together at the Invictus Games in Toronto, Canada. Her engagement to Prince Harry was announced on 27th November 2017, which prompted another announcement that Meghan would retirement from acting with the intention to pursue humanitarian work. The engagement announcement prompted much comment about Meghan becoming a proudly mixed-race member of the Royal Family.

Harry created a bespoke engagement ring for Meghan which was designed and forged with a large central diamond from Botswana and two smaller diamonds from the jewellery collection of his late mother. Meghan has since been baptised into the Anglican faith and is currently going through the process of becoming a British citizen.

Diana, Princess of Wales
(1961 – 1997)

- 50 ml infused gin with lavender
- 25 ml homemade passion fruit syrup
- 15 ml egg white
- 20 ml lemon juice
- violet liqueur and flower, to garnish

Method: Keep that Martini shaker handy and mix all of the ingredients together with ice. Shake completely until ice chips have formed and double strain into a thin crystal Martini glass.

Delicately place an edible violet flower in the centre of the cocktail with three drops of violet liqueur placed around the flower.

Interesting Facts:

Lady Diana Frances Spencer, or Diana, Princess of Wales as she was known, was the youngest daughter of John Spencer, Viscount Althorp, and Frances Roche. She was the first wife of Prince Charles, The Prince of Wales to whom was born Prince William, Duke of Cambridge and Prince Henry (Harry) of Wales, the Duke of Sussex. Born on 1st July 1961, Diana was of British nobility with Royal ancestry. Diana's family hold the titles of Duke of

Marlborough, Earl Spencer, Earl of Sunderland, and Baron Churchill of Whichwood. Diana and Charles were distantly related, as they were both descended from the House of Tudor through Henry VII of England. Diana was also directly descended from the House of Stuart through Charles II of England by Charles Lennox, 1st Duke of Richmond, and Henry FitzRoy, 1st Duke of Grafton, and his brother James II of England by Henrietta FitzJames. Diana's American lineage came from her great-grandmother Frances Ellen Work, the daughter of wealthy American stockbroker Franklin H. Work from Ohio, who was married to her great-grandfather James Roche, the 3rd Baron Fermoy.

Diana's wedding to Charles, Prince of Wales took place at St Paul's Cathedral on 29th July 1981. Over 750 million people around the world tuned in to watch the wedding on the television. During her marriage, Diana was not just Princess of Wales, but also the Duchess of Cornwall, Duchess of Rothesay, and the Countess of Chester. As a senior member of the Royal Family, Diana undertook royal duties on behalf of the Queen and represented her at functions overseas. She was celebrated for her charity work and for her unwavering support of the International Campaign to Ban Landmines. She was further involved with dozens of charities including London's Great Ormond Street Hospital for Children, of which she was their President from 1989. Diana used her worldwide celebrity status to raise awareness and advocate ways to help people affected with HIV/AIDS, cancer, and mental illness.

Among members of the Royal Family throughout history, Diana remains one of the most popular, and continues to influence the principles of the Royal Family and its younger generations through her two children who carry on her legacy through their own charity works. Since her untimely death in the summer of 1997, Diana has been remembered for her charisma, compassion, style, and high-profile charity work, whilst being mostly remembered for her encounters with sick and dying patients, the poor and the unwanted. In a 1995 interview, Diana stated that she would like to be, "a queen of people's hearts, in people's hearts."

Thank you!

We would like to express our thanks to M Den, M Wine and M Restaurants for their help and support in the creation of the cocktails featured in the *A Royal Line-Up*, *A Right Royal Tipple*, and *A Royal Finale* chapters.

After a full decade travelling the globe, dining at the finest restaurants, visiting vineyards, drinking in cocktail bars and staying in hotels in the search for inspiring hospitality, Martin Williams' inspirations germinated into the creation of M. The resources and energy expended ended up being shrewd investments. All of the places he'd spent time in contributed to the story, making it compelling. M, in short, is borne on the shoulders of its inspirations and Martin's imagination.

Ask Martin and the philosophy of M is quite simple. It is to bring the highest-quality food, beverage and hospitality offerings possible to his guests. At M, this goes as far as being able to use the M website to choose your own table in 'airline style' before you dine – an industry first. On a local scale, Martin is passionate about the multiculturalism of London and wanted to create a restaurant that is a true mirror of cultural liberalism. M draws inspiration from  international cuisines, but it's also supported by an international team of staff, many of whom learned their trade in some of the foremost eateries and venues across the planet. M isn't simply a restaurant or a bar, it's closer to a private members' club or hotel in feel, and the type of venue that you'd use for a range of purposes. The success of M has been predicated on fostering relationships with regulars who return almost daily.

www.mrestaurants.co.uk

After leaving the Italian Navy, Lorenz Tullio Santonocito, of M Den, M Wine and M Restaurants, moved from Sicily to London ten years ago. Working in central London restaurants, he developed an interest in the art of cocktail making and mixology, to which he became a bartender a short time later. As a barkeep, he started to experiment with cocktails at home and would bring his ideas to work. Creating cocktail after cocktail and adding them to his repertoire, his wonderful liquid concoctions were met with great enthusiasm and superb ratings.

Over the years, Tullio has worked his way up the service industry ladder to attain a Restaurant Director position with M, whilst still maintaining his love of mixology. Having never relinquished his love of cocktails or his exceptional ability to create them, Tullio welcomed the opportunity to come on board with this publication, accepting the challenge to create new and exciting celebratory cocktails in honour of the Blue Sapphire Jubilee of Her Majesty The Queen and the centenary of the House of Windsor.

Tullio came to this project with an imposing mantra and a discerning belief that creating aesthetically pleasing cocktails, which excite the palate, are your first introduction to over a decade of his work. He is a strong believer of first impressions and hopes that when you try one of his creations, that you are pleased, satisfied and put at ease. Tullio sincerely hopes that you enjoy this book and the many cocktail recipes that he has created especially for this project. He challenges you to try at least one or two of these fantastic cocktails from the recipes contained within this book and to further visit M in one of their three locations to sample an extensive list of cocktails he has created.

M Bar

It's hard to nail down inspirations for a bar, particularly when you're operating in one of the best markets for cocktail bars on the planet. Three international bars that figured into the psyche of M are The Bar & Courtyard at the Setai in Miami, Floreria Atlantico in Buenos Aires and a strange little bolt-hole in Tokyo that Martin can only nebulously recollect.

The bar at M is eminently adaptable: guests can pop up and have a glass of wine – or indeed a flight – be led on a wine tasting by a sommelier, enjoy a cocktail, a pint of lager, or open a bottle of champagne. It's both accessible and aspirational; diners can choose to eat the big M burger or caviar, as well as anything in between. The only important benchmark is that the dish is playful. This extends to the cocktail list which was put together by the bar team, overseen by Restaurant Director Lorenz Tullio Santonocito and Operations Director André Mannini. Together, they constructed a drinks list that consistently subverts expectations. Just as in M Grill and M Raw, guests will initially be struck by the flavour of the drink, before the cocktail's texture, mouthfeel or garnish supplies a secondary surprise.

M Bar also shares common blood with the restaurants in that it uses the finest ingredients. All of the house spirits are premium brands: the vodka is Belvedere; the gin is Tanqueray 10; rum is Ron Zacapa; even the vermouth is top-shelf – Cocchi Americano. No punches are pulled in assuring that drinkers are sipping the best.

M Victoria: Zig Zag Building, 74 Victoria St, London SW1E 6SQ
M Threadneedle Street: Unit 2-3, 60 Threadneedle St, London EC2R 8HP
M Twickenham: 1 Brewery Lane, Twickenham TW1 1AA
mrestaurants.co.uk

From Her Majesty's Kitchen

A fine pairing of canapés by
Mr Robert Kennedy, Former Executive Chef, Royal Military Academy Sandhurst

As an Executive Chef in Defence Catering, Rob is based at the world famous Royal Military Academy Sandhurst. Rob is no stranger to working at the highest culinary tier. His exciting chef career has seen him develop and serve up "Great British Menus" for celebrities and Royal international dignitaries. Rob has cooked for Her Majesty The Queen five times at prestige events, including the Sovereign's Parade for the Royal Princes and the 2012 Diamond Jubilee at Windsor Castle.

Rob's passionate and enthusiastic character is empathised in his dishes, which are described as "classic recipes with a modern exciting twist". Rob's love for food started as a young boy working on his grandparent's farm, helping his grandmother in the kitchen. Rob is at the peak of his culinary career and has already twice represented Compass UK and Ireland at The Culinary Olympic Games in Germany, bringing home both Gold and Silver medals. These accolades are part of a long line of 85 culinary awards Rob has achieved in the last ten years. Rob has been nominated top three in the country, in three different categories at the UK Craft Guild of Chefs Awards, winning Cost Sector Chef of the Year in 2010. Rob is currently a member of The National Culinary Team of England, representing his country at the Culinary World Cup in 2016. He won the silver medal for Prestige dining for HM British Forces.

Royal Canapés

Fine Royal foods to compliment fresh and exciting Royal drinks
By Chef Robert Kennedy

This book blends a large component of modern British culture with the historic ties and research of fashionable blends and drinks. However, this is only half the story when enjoying cocktails, as there is the golden rule: "eat and treat". Throughout our British history, food is at the core of any Royal celebration. Therefore, let's consider the perfect pairing for our Royal cocktails; some tasty Royal canapés.

Royal canapés have been an active and vital component to Royal entertaining with seventeen thousand of the little savouries served for the wedding celebrations of His Royal Highness The Prince of Wales to Camilla Parker Bowles at Windsor Castle in 2005. A further ten thousand were served at Buckingham Palace during the wedding celebrations of his son, Prince William to Miss Catherine Middleton in 2011. Royal events encounter prestige dining which have outlined the modern form of banquets we now see at the many State Visits and receptions held at Buckingham Palace and Windsor Castle. Food is a culture and with great pride and passion, we can deliver perfection. Simple ingredients married together to produce bite-size delights is a perfect and traditional way to start any banquet or special occasion.

As Executive Chef of the Royal Military Academy Sandhurst, I have had the privilege and honour of cooking for Her Majesty a total of five times. Two memorable occasions were the running of the Royal Box for Her Majesty The Queen's Diamond Jubilee and her 90th birthday celebrations at Windsor Castle. Included in my career, I have also cooked for many inward State Visits of international Royal families, senior dignitaries and world leaders.

During my time at Sandhurst, it has been a honour and pleasure going into work every day. The diverse cooking of high-end quality has made my culinary journey unforgettable, educational and honourable. In 2006, Prince Harry and Prince William completed a full year at Sandhurst. To celebrate the completion of their commissioning course, I designed the Sovereign's Lunch Menu. Both the Royal lunches included immediate Royal Family and the event catered for 1,200 guests.

Having served Her Majesty and members of our Royal Family through my culinary career, I also work for numerous charities and have raised over £50,000 in my spare time for such great and worthwhile causes. A couple of the charities I support include Help for Heroes, Ups and Downs, and Children In Need. My inspiration for food and the creation associated with its preparation and cooking has seen me as a Chef Presenter for seven years, where I continue to work at many UK food shows demonstrating my own recipes and modern style of cooking. Sharing simple recipes, which can easily be produced at home or the work place, is an important message to support our nation's exciting culinary journey. As a chef, I have collected over 85 national and international culinary awards, which includes two Chef of the Year titles, two culinary Oscars and two World Olympic Gold medals. I have been a Member of the National England Culinary Team since 2014 and I regularly judge at national United Kingdom culinary competitions and hospitality shows, including the London Excel and NEC Birmingham.

As a chef, it is important that time, strength and energy is provided for the young, up-and-coming future chefs of our industry. The day-to-day running of the kitchens and the hosting of prestige dinners help to inspire and excite our apprentices. It is a real pleasure to see the enthusiasm and development that the chefs gain from delivering many of the big functions and Royal events. Like the research in this book, which represents an era in time of the history of this nation, I can appreciate the work, dedication and time put into the documentation of this interesting subject of research for the reader's enjoyment.

Much like Thomas has researched and documented his Royal subjects, I can see his passion and so I jumped at the chance to provide a handful of great recipes to accompany the many wonderful drinks within this book. Like Thomas, I enjoy a good gin and tonic or a glass of red wine, over which countless conversations with him have been had. We have in common the desire to create and share Royal history, fun cocktails and delicious canapés recipes. I trust that you will enjoy the fine pairing of Royal foods together with the many interesting drinks that are presented within this book.

I have loved cooking from a young age, when I would watch and help my Nanny Wyn with her baking. Every week, we would travel to the family farm in Cambridgeshire. I can remember watching and learning all the old-fashioned recipes, which later developed an inspiration for me to move into the professional kitchen. My food style has become excitable and passionate. It resembles simple flavours presented with a modern "good-looking" fashion. It's great to eat small food and experience your favourite memories. These delicious canapés offer etiquette and pleasure to showcase tasty culinary treasures. Bite-size food can just be picked up, served on a spoon or carefully arranged on tasty crunchy bread. Enjoy these delicious bite-size gems that marry wonderful with the following drinks. Bon appétit!

Chef Robert Kennedy

Rare Fillet Steak and Onions with a Horseradish Mayonnaise

"A real British tradition from Sunday roast to the perfect pre-dinner treat"

The Shopping List for 10

- 150 g beef fillet steak, seasoned
- drizzle of olive oil
- knob of butter
- 2 garlic cloves, chopped
- 1 tsp horseradish sauce
- 2 tsp mayonnaise
- good sprig of thyme and tarragon leaves
- 1 brioche finger roll

In the Kitchen

Season the fillet steak and pan sear with thyme and garlic over a high heat in oil and butter. Cook for a total of one minute until roasted and brown in colour. The centre needs to remain pink and rare. Rest for 5 minutes, then place into the fridge for 30 minutes. Cut your brioche into thin slices and place onto a foiled tray. Bake at 165°C for 3 minutes. Remove and leave to go cool and crunchy. Mix together the mayonnaise and horseradish sauce, spoon onto the brioche toast, thinly slice the beef and roll into bite-size pieces. Place onto the toast and garnish with more horseradish and fresh tarragon leaves.

Watermelon and Feta

"This is a great dish for the summer and very similar to what I prepared for The Countess of Wessex!"

The Shopping List for 10

- 1 medium watermelon (plenty leftovers left for breakfast)
- 3 tsp balsamic glaze
- 50 g feta cheese
- 1 tsp chopped walnuts
- good pinch small basil leaves

In the Kitchen

Slice the watermelon into 20 mm slices, carefully removing the seeds, and dice into even 20 mm cubes. Use a melon scoop to make a small cavity into the top of each one. Add a drizzle of balsamic glaze and crumble the delicious feta on top. Finish with chopped walnuts and delicate small bunches of basil leaves.

Roast Salmon, Honey Crème Fraîche and Peas

"Simple flavours to gather succulent fish with sticky sweet honey and crunchy toast. Salmon is very popular in our restaurants and I have previously used it as a starter for Her Majesty The Queen."

The Shopping List for 10

- 150 g salmon, seasoned
- 3 tsp crème fraîche
- 2 tsp clear honey
- 1 tsp lemon juice
- 1 brioche finger roll
- handful shelled peas and pea shoots

In the Kitchen

Place your salmon fillet onto a foiled baking tray, season and drizzle with a little olive oil and fresh lemon juice. Roast for 10 minutes at 170°C in a pre-heated oven. Remove and brush the salmon with clear honey and rest at room temperature for 30 minutes. Cut your brioche into thin slices and place onto a foiled tray. Bake at 165°C for 3 minutes. Remove and leave to go cool and crunchy. Spoon the crème fraîche onto the toast and place small pieces of the salmon on top. Drizzle with clear honey and decorate with shelled peas and pea shoot herbs.

Peeled Cucumber, Minted Guacamole and Lentil Sprouts

"For the healthy tempting textures of chilled cucumber, smooth guacamole and lentil sprouts, this one works great and ticks all the boxes."

The Shopping List for 10

- half a cucumber
- 3 tbsp guacamole
- 1 tsp mint sauce
- fresh mint sprigs
- 30 g lentil sprout mix

In the Kitchen

Peel the cucumber and cut into small cylinder 25 mm discs. Mix the mint sauce with the guacamole. Neatly pipe on top of the cucumber. Garnish with the tasty lentil sprouts and fresh mint sprigs.

Roast Chicken and Mango

"Traditional roast chicken sweetened up with juicy fresh mango. This recipe offers clean presentation with a very refreshing flavour."

The Shopping List for 10

- 100 g roast chicken
- 50 g fresh mango
- 1 spring onion
- 1 chive
- 1 brioche finger roll
- 3 tsp mayonnaise
- 1 tsp mango chutney

In the Kitchen

Slice the mango into even neat ribbons. Thinly slice the spring onion into small discs. Cut your brioche into thin slices and place onto a foiled tray, then bake at 165°C for 3 minutes. Remove and leave to go cool and crunchy. Mix the mayonnaise with mango chutney and blend to a smooth dressing. Slice your cooked chicken breast into small bite-size nuggets. Spread the mango onto the brioche, then place the chicken on top. Garnish with fresh mango, spring onion and fresh chive.

English Asparagus Spears and Soft Quail Egg

"Showcasing our finesse with English asparagus and a soft boiled egg. One simple bite from the etiquette of a china serving spoon."

The Shopping List for 10

- 10 small asparagus spears
- 5 quail eggs
- 3 baby tomatoes
- 3 tbsp cream cheese

In the Kitchen

Remove asparagus roots and blanch remanding spears in salted boiling water for 30 seconds. Refresh in ice-cold water. Boil quail egg for 2 minutes and 40 seconds, then place into cold water. Remove the shell of the quail egg. Pipe the cream cheese onto a serving spoon, slice the asparagus spearheads in half lengthways and build neatly on top. Cut the soft quail egg in half, and place on top of the cream cheese. Add a slice of baby tomato for extra flavour and colour.

Sausage and Mash with Onion Relish

"Hot, yummy, retro English food looking posh and tasty. One of my most popular bite-size offers for pre-dinner drinks and garden parties."

The Shopping List for 10

- 3 chipolata sausages
- 1 baking potato
- knob of butter, approx 25 g
- splash of milk
- 1 banana shallot or small onion, finely diced
- 1 tsp soft brown sugar
- 3 tbsp red wine vinegar
- 1 tbsp soy sauce
- chives, chopped, to garnish

In the Kitchen

Boil the potato until soft and tender, strain and dry, then mash together with milk, butter and seasoning. Pan fry your sausages in a little vegetable oil until golden brown, remove and place into a pre-heated oven at 165°C for 5 minutes. Add the onions into your frying pan and cook until caramelised and soft. Add red wine vinegar, soy sauce and sugar; continue cooking for one minute. Serve on a presenting spoon the creamy mash, a slice of sausage and sticky onion dressing. Finish with a sprinkle of finely chopped chives.

Sweet and Sour Duck

The Shopping List for 10

- 4 duck breasts
- half a cucumber
- 4 radishes
- 2 banana shallots
- 100 g green seedless grapes
- fennel herb or mustard cress, to garnish
- 1 vanilla pod
- 75 ml clear honey
- 1 tsp stem ginger root syrup from jar
- 200 ml white wine vinegar
- 125 g caster sugar
- 1 star anise
- 5 cardamom pods
- small cinnamon stick
- 2 large parsnips
- 1 pint milk
- 75 g salted butter
- Maldon sea salt
- 25 ml soy sauce
- 25 ml bitter orange liqueur

In the Kitchen

Duck breast

Trim any excess sinew from underneath the duck breast. Score the top fat closely together. Season the duck and place skin down in a cold pan over a moderate heat for about 4 to 5 minutes. Press gently down onto the duck breast to ensure it remains flat. When the duck fat has rendered and the skin is golden brown and crispy to the touch, turn the breast over once. Fry for a further 20 seconds using the excess duck fat to baste and flavour. Place into an oven with the skin side up for 5 minutes at 180°C. Remove duck and rest for a further 5 minutes before dicing.

Pickle liquor and salad garnish
Bring the white wine vinegar, sugar and spice to the boil and leave to cool. Peel and char the cucumber with a blow torch and then portion into small batons. Thinly slice the radish and shallot rings, half the green grapes and place in cold pickle for 5 minutes to flavour.

Smoked Parsnip butter cream
Peel and smoke the parsnips slowly over apple wood or oak for 90 minutes. Dice the parsnip into 1 inch (2 cm) cubes. Place into milk and boil until tender.

Remove and place into a hand blender cylinder, adding chilled butter and a little of the smoky parsnip milk. Blend until smooth and creamy.

Dressing and garnish
Mix clear honey with bitter orange and soya sauce. Add vanilla seeds from pod. Whisk together with a little of the stem ginger syrup. Baste sticky dressing over the duck when removed from oven and resting. Garnish with fennel herb for flavour.

Plate
Spoon the parsnip butter cream onto the plate, evenly arranging the pickles, add the duck, slicing into four pieces, and finish with a drizzle of dressing, crunchy radish and delicate herbs.

By Appointment to
HM The Queen

A Right Royal Tipple

A selection of tasty tipples in celebration of the longest reigning and most celebrated sovereign in British history.

Presented in part by:

**Wilkin & Sons Tiptree
By Appointment to Her Majesty The Queen**

Cheers to The Queen

- 12 ml gin
- 12 ml Dubonnet
- 12 ml English Damson Gin Liqueur
- 1 tsp ginger liqueur
- twisted lime peel, to garnish

Method: Turning to our trusted Martini shaker, combine the above listed ingredients and shake vigorously with ice until ice chips are formed in the mixture. Pour into a cut crystal Martini glass, garnish with a twisted lime peel and enjoy.

FUN FACT

In 1324, during King Edward II's reign, a statute proclaimed sturgeon, porpoise, whale, and dolphin as 'Fishes Royal'. This means that today The Queen technically owns them and when they are caught within three miles (about five km) off British shores or washed up, they may be claimed on behalf of the Crown. As a rule of thumb, when "Fishes Royal" are brought into port, a sturgeon is sold in the usual way, and the purchaser, as a gesture of loyalty, requests the honour of its being accepted by HM Queen Elizabeth II.

The Quintessentially English

- 40 ml gin
- 10 ml lemon juice
- 10 ml elderflower sugar
- 10 ml Chartreuse Green Liqueur
- 4 mint leaves, to garnish
- 3 slices cucumber, to garnish

Method: In that well-used Martini shaker, muddle the cucumber with gin. Clap the mint to release aroma and oils, then add to the shaker. Combine and shake the ingredients with ice until ice chips form. Double strain into a thin, crystal Martini glass. Garnish with cucumber and mint to enjoy this cool refreshment on a hot English summer's afternoon.

FUN FACT

In 1998, Her Majesty The Queen surprised King Abdullah of Saudi Arabia (at the time Crown Prince) by driving him around in her country estate of Balmoral in her Land Rover. Former British Ambassador to Saudi Arabia, Sir Sherard Cowper-Coles, describes this motor tour of Balmoral by Her Majesty:

"As instructed, the Crown Prince climbed into the front seat of the front Land Rover, with his interpreter in the seat behind. To his surprise, The Queen climbed into the driving seat, turned the ignition and drove off. Women are not — yet — allowed to drive in Saudi Arabia, and Abdullah was not used to being driven by a woman, let alone a queen. His (The Crown Prince's) nervousness only increased as The Queen, an army driver in wartime, accelerated the Land Rover along the narrow Scottish estate roads, talking all the time. Through his interpreter, the Crown Prince implored The Queen to slow down and concentrate on the road ahead."

The Joking Duke of Edinburgh

- 40 ml gin
- 4 drops ANGOSTURA® aromatic bitters
- 10 ml lime juice
- 10 ml Smoked Water
- 4 drops of ANGOSTURA® orange bitters
- twisted lime peel, to garnish

Method: Rinse out that Martini shaker because here we go again! Combine and shake the aforementioned ingredients with ice until your hands are borderline frostbitten. Double strain into a crystal tulip glass, garnish with a twist of lime, and enjoy repeatedly. Eventually, any and every joke will be amusing!

FUN FACT

The Queen has her own personal poet. The honorary position of "Poet Laureate" is granted by Her Majesty to a poet "whose work is of national significance". When this privileged position was introduced, the "Poet Laureate" was paid £200 per year plus a butt of canary wine. Today, they receive a barrel of sherry. Ms. Carol Ann Duffy will hold this prized position until the year 2019.

Balmoral Pride

- 25 ml gin
- 25 ml dessert wine
- 10 ml lemon juice
- 10 ml violet liqueur
- 15 ml hibiscus liqueur
- tangerine twist, to garnish

Method: In our Martini shaker, shake all of the ingredients together – no ice. Pour into a large white wine glass over ice and garnish with a tangerine twist, and enjoy the cool reflections of Her Majesty's famous Highland home.

FUN FACT

The Queen has the power to create Knights and appoint Peers (Lords) to sit in Parliament in the House of Lords. When it comes to laws, The Queen's consent is necessary to turn any Bill, that has passed through Parliament, into an actual law. The Bill is placed into the famed "Red Box" and sent for Her Majesty's approval. This is called "Royal Assent". The most recent British monarch to refuse "Royal Assent" was Queen Anne, back in 1708.

The Jewel of Windsor

- 40 ml gin
- 10 ml raspberry gin liqueur
- 12 ml elderflower liqueur
- 12 ml King's Ginger Liqueur
- 12 ml sugar syrup
- 12 ml lemon juice
- splash of Windsor Great Park English Sparkling Wine

Method: In a clean Martini shaker, combine and shake the aforementioned ingredients (with the exception of the English sparkling wine) with ice until frothy and cold. Pour into a proper champagne saucer and top up with Windsor Great Park English Sparkling Wine. Here you will have the proper cocktail to toast Her Majesty: "The Queen!"

FUN FACT

Her Majesty is not obliged to pay any form of tax within her kingdom. However, she has been voluntarily paying income tax and capital gains tax since her 'Annus Horribilis' of 1992.

Her Majesty's Commonwealth

- 20 ml Campari
- 10 ml rye whiskey
- 4 drops barrel aged whiskey bitter
- 10 ml apple liqueur
- orange peel, to garnish

Method: In a clean mixing glass, combine the aforementioned ingredients and swizzle gently. Pour directly into a rocks glass over ice and garnish with a few orange peels to create a rose.

FUN FACT

Whilst many of The Queen's prerogative powers are devolved to either her government ministers, there is an exception which allows her to exercise real power by herself. "In grave constitutional crisis," the sovereign can "act contrary to or without Ministerial advice." Therefore, Her Majesty can in fact overrule and ignore ministerial advice and act as she sees fit.

A Summer Sapphire Jubilee

- 40 ml rye whiskey
- 20 ml sweet vermouth
- 20 ml Amaro Averna
- 10 ml Campari
- 15 ml blue Curaçao
- 2 drops of ANGOSTURA® orange bitters
- thyme, to garnish

Method: In a crystal mixing glass, combine and stir the ingredients with ice until cold. Strain into a crystal coupe, garnish with thyme and enjoy.

FUN FACT

The Marquis of Ailesbury is a Hereditary Warden of Savernake Forest and is required to produce a blast on a hunting horn should the sovereign pass through the Forest. This last happened in 1943 during the reign of King George VI.

To date, wax museum Madame Tussauds have displayed 23 different life-size models of Her Majesty The Queen.

The Duchess of Edinburgh

- 40 ml gin
- 10 ml cucumber syrup
- a few dashes of orange essence
- elderflower lemonade
- cucumber, to garnish
- mint, to garnish

Method: In a white wine glass, combine the gin, cucumber syrup and orange essence over balls of ice. Top up with elderflower lemonade. Give a gentle swizzle and garnish with a cucumber and mint.

FUN FACT

For one week each year, The Queen stays in Edinburgh at Holyrood Palace. The Scottish variant of the Royal Standard of the United Kingdom is flown above the Palace but at all other times the Royal Banner of Scotland is displayed. During The Queen's visits, the Royal Company of Archers form her ceremonial bodyguard.

Caernarfon's Queen

- 50 ml white tequila
- 15 ml Briolette Basil
- 15 ml Triple Sec
- 25 ml lime juice
- 4-5 fresh basil leaves, to garnish

Method: Warm up that Martini shaker (not literally)! Combine and shake the ingredients with ice until frosty cold. Strain into a Martini glass, garnish with a basil leaf.

FUN FACT

On 25th April 1284, Edward I's son, Edward was born in Caernarfon Castle. The Welsh people wanted to have a prince of their own, one that was born in Wales and could speak neither English nor French. He must speak Welsh. The Barons went to The King with their request. The King agreed and then brought out his infant son Edward, declaring him their first Prince of Wales. He was born in Wales and he could speak neither English nor French but would learn Welsh.

The Windsor Great Park

- 50 ml gin
- 12.5 ml grapefruit juice
- 12.5 ml sugar syrup
- 1 dash apricot liqueur
- splash of Windsor Great Park English Sparkling Wine
- mint, to garnish
- apricot, to garnish

Method: In a clean Martini shaker, combine and shake the aforementioned ingredients (without the sparkling wine) with ice. Pour into a champagne goblet and top up with Windsor Great Park English Sparkling Wine. Garnish with mint held together with apricot skin ties.

FUN FACT

The Duke of Wellington pays rent to Her Majesty by way of presenting a French Tricolour flag before noon on 18th June, the anniversary of the Battle of Waterloo. This private ceremony is held at Windsor Castle.

Her Hillsborough Highness

- 40 ml gin
- 10 ml raspberry gin liqueur
- 5 ml lemon juice
- 5 ml balsamic vinegar
- 2 fresh raspberries, to garnish
- 4 mint leaves

Method: Muddle the strawberries with lemon juice and mint in our trusty Martini shaker. Add all ingredients from above with the exception of the raspberries, shake vigorously and double strain into a large red wine bowl over ice. Garnish with raspberries and enjoy.

FUN FACT

The modern Royal history of Hillsborough Castle began in the 1920s when leading members of the Royal Family began to use it as their de facto Royal Residence in Northern Ireland. The first meeting between The Queen and Mary McAleese, then President of Ireland, occurred at Hillsborough in 2005. The Prince of Wales held an investiture at Hillsborough Castle in 2014 which was the first one to be held there since it became a Royal Palace.

The Merry Prince

- 40 ml tequila
- 15 ml Cointreau
- 15 ml lime juice
- 10 ml Aperol
- 10 ml Grand Marnier
- orange twist, to garnish

Method: Our Martini shaker gets to meet a Martini glass this time. Shake all the ingredients together in the shaker and double strain into the Martini glass. Garnish with an orange twist.

FUN FACT

Her Majesty must consent in advance for a debate to take place in Parliament on any law which could affect the interests of the Crown, the monarch or her family. This is called "Queen's Consent". This has been exercised 39 times, always on the advice of The Queen's ministers. The Guardian newspaper reported on one instance where Her Majesty used her veto power in 1999 against "the Military Actions Against Iraq Bill. This was a private member's bill that sought to transfer the power to authorise military strikes against Iraq from the monarch to Parliament".

BY THE KING.

A PROCLAMATION

Declaring that the Name of Windsor is to be borne by His Royal House and Family and relinquishing the use of all German Titles and Dignities.

GEORGE R.I.

WHEREAS WE, having taken into consideration the Name and Title of Our Royal House and Family, have determined that henceforth Our House and Family shall be styled and known as the House and Family of Windsor:

AND WHEREAS We have further determined for Ourselves and for and on behalf of Our descendants and all other the descendants of Our Grandmother Queen Victoria of blessed and glorious memory to relinquish and discontinue the use of all German Titles and Dignities:

AND WHEREAS We have declared these Our determinations in Our Privy Council:

NOW, THEREFORE, We, out of Our Royal Will and Authority, do hereby declare and announce that as from the date of this Our Royal Proclamation Our House and Family shall be styled and known as the House and Family of Windsor, and that all the descendants in the male line of Our said Grandmother Queen Victoria who are subjects of these Realms, other than female descendants who may marry or may have married, shall bear the said Name of Windsor:

And do hereby further declare and announce that We for Ourselves and for and on behalf of Our descendants and all other the descendants of Our said Grandmother Queen Victoria who are subjects of these Realms, relinquish and enjoin the discontinuance of the use of the Degrees, Styles, Dignities, Titles and Honours of Dukes and Duchesses of Saxony and Princes and Princesses of Saxe-Coburg and Gotha, and all other German Degrees, Styles, Dignities, Titles, Honours and Appellations to Us or to them heretofore belonging or appertaining.

Given at Our Court at Buckingham Palace, this Seventeenth day of July, in the year of our Lord One thousand nine hundred and seventeen, and in the Eighth year of Our Reign.

GOD SAVE THE KING.

Windsor By Royal Proclamation

The Centenary of Britain's Royal House
1917 - 2017

It is no secret that the British Royal Family has deeply seeded German roots. German George I became the first monarch of the House of Hanover in the United Kingdom following The Act of Settlement of 1701. This stated that no Catholic could ascent the British throne so, with the death of Queen Anne in 1714, her distant second cousin George was the closest Protestant in line. This enraged the Scottish Jacobites, who believed that Anne's Catholic half-brother, James Stuart, should take the throne. This led to the Jacobite uprisings and eventually to the defeat of their cause in 1746 at the Battle of Culloden.

King George I of Great Britain did not speak English and spent considerable time in Hanover where he retained his titles and lands. The German connections were strengthened by Royal marriages including Queen Victoria's beloved husband, Albert, who was from the House of Saxe-Coburg and Gotha.

Reacting to anti-German sentiment in the British Empire during World War I and cognisant of the demise of several European dynastic monarchies, including the Russian Royal Family, King George V decided to act. He not only abandoned the German name of his family, but also relinquished all titles and privileges associated with it. The House of Windsor was born.

King George died during one of his many visits to Hanover on 11th June 1727. He was succeeded by his son who became George II, King of Great Britain and Ireland, The Duke of Brunswick-Lüneburg and prince-elector of the Holy Roman Empire. The newly ascended King, who had been born and raised in Hanover, was the last British sovereign to be born abroad. George II decided not to attend his father's funeral in Hanover. This decision went down very well with his British subjects who saw it as a sign that he put his duties to Great Britain first. He spent 12 summers in Hanover overseeing his obligations to his people there, out of the 33 (nearly one in three) he had as King George II. He was a brave soldier who fought in the European wars over the Austrian succession; he himself led the British army into battle at Dettingen and won a great victory. It was the final time that a British king personally fought in battle. His reign saw the ultimate defeat of the Stuart cause when Charles Edward Stuart (Bonnie Prince Charlie), grandson of James II, was beaten at Culloden Moor. It also saw the extension of British influence and territories in India and what is now Canada.

George II's son died in 1751, leaving his grandson to become George III of Great Britain and Ireland on 25th October 1760. Although both of his parents were German, he had been born – the first of the Hanoverian Kings to have been – in England. He spoke English as his first language and never visited Hanover, the land of his forefathers. British through and through, George III was dearly loved by his subjects as one of their own. He was unpretentious and when out riding or walking in the fields, he would speak to those he met and take an interest in what they were doing. Often called the "Farmer King", he was interested in agriculture and had a wonderful ability to relate to ordinary people. George was a kind man and dutiful king.

Though there were many turbulent episodes during his kingship, such as his personal health, familial discord, and the loss of Britain's American colonies, his long reign encompassed great achievements in the arts, the sciences and in military matters, culminating in the defeat of the French Emperor Napoleon at Waterloo in 1815. Britain became the dominant nation in Europe; with her army and navy feared and respected, the country was inexorably positioned to become a superpower during the reign of Empire.

George III's reign and life were longer than that of any previous monarch. He celebrated a Golden Jubilee and, after 57 years on the throne, died at Windsor Castle on 29th January 1820. He was succeeded by his son and regent, King George IV. When George IV's brother and successor expired without legitimate issue, the British throne went to his niece Victoria, and the immediate link with Hanover was broken. Salic law prevented a woman from being Hanover's ruler.

The name Windsor has been associated with royalty in Britain for nearly one thousand years. Windsor began as a fortress and evolved into a grand palace, beloved by successive kings and queens. The castle and the surrounding town have become a treasured British icon. It was this town and Royal residence which were chosen by King George V to rebrand his family's image. The decision followed an escalation of events. In March 1917, anti-German sentiment amongst the British people reached a new high when, still in the early days of air warfare, the German-made Gotha G4 aircraft crossed the channel and began bombing England, and London in particular. This heavy enemy aircraft, which bore the name of our Royal House, was a glaring reminder to the population of the Royal Family's ties to a foreign and hostile nation. It was during this tense time that trouble advanced from the east of Germany as well as from the west. On 15th March, King George V's cousin, Czar Nicholas II of Russia, was forced to abdicate his throne. This cataclysmic abdication threatened the stability and very existence of every Royal House in Europe. Fearing the worst, on the advice of his minsters, King George V made the decision to relinquish all of the titles accustomed to him and his family under the German Crown. The King proceeded to change such titles and names to their English counterparts. Between 1917 and 1919, King George V took further steps to show that his ties to Germany were nothing more than cosmetic and stripped over a dozen of his German family members of their British titles and styles of Prince and Princess.

By Royal proclamation, the name of the British Royal Family was changed from Saxe-Coburg and Gotha to Windsor on 17th July 1917. The Royal Proclamation read: "Now, therefore, We, out of Our Royal Will and Authority, do hereby declare and announce that as from the date of this Our Royal Proclamation Our House and Family shall

Windsor Castle.
Photo: Thomas Mace-Archer-Mills.

be styled and known as the House and Family of Windsor, and that all the descendants in the male line of Our said Grandmother Queen Victoria who are subjects of these Realms, other than female descendants who may marry or may have married, shall bear the said Name of Windsor."

As per the Royal Proclamation of 1917 and by the year 1919, the living male line of the British descendants of Queen Victoria subject to British rule were King George V; his five sons; his daughter, Princess Mary; his sister, Princess Victoria; his uncle, Prince Arthur, The Duke of Connaught and Strathearn; his cousin, Prince Arthur of Connaught, his cousin, Prince Alastair of Connaught (once removed), and his cousin, Princess Patricia of Connaught. Prince Alastair of Connaught and Princess Victoria never married and died without issue. Princess Mary wed into the Lascelles family, while Princess Patricia married a commoner, Mr Alexander Ramsay. Neither of the Connaught men produced any further male issue which cemented the line of subsequent male heirs of the House of Windsor to descend from Prince Albert, The Duke of York (King George VI), Prince Henry, The Duke of Gloucester, and Prince George, The Duke of Kent. Prince John expired in 1919 from an epileptic seizure at the age of 13 and the briefly reigning Edward VIII, later The Duke of Windsor, was childless.

The abdication crisis instigated by Edward VIII in 1936 when he married the divorcee Wallis Simpson, threatened to disrupt the Royal Proclamation of his father. Since the reign of Queen Victoria, there had always been a male heir to carry on the family name but with King Edward VIII having no issue, King George VI faced a dilemma. He had girls. On 20th November 1947, Princess Elizabeth married Philip Mountbatten at Westminster Abbey, London. Philip, who was a Prince of Greece and Denmark in his own right, belonged to the House of Schleswig-Holstein-Sonderburg-Glücksburg, which is a branch of the German House of Oldenburg. It was suggested, and subsequently enacted, that Prince Philip relinquish all his foreign Royal titles and adopt his maternal uncle's name of Mountbatten prior to his wedding to Princess Elizabeth. Philip's uncle and mentor, The Earl Mountbatten of Burma, was himself a product of the Royal Proclamation of 1917, as the surname "Mountbatten" had been assumed by Lord Mountbatten's father, Prince Louis of Battenberg. Mountbatten is the anglicised name of the German town of Battenberg.

Not long after Princess Elizabeth became Queen in February 1952, Prince Philip and Lord Mountbatten urged The Queen to adopt the name "Mountbatten" as the new name of her Royal House, since it was customary for a wife to adopt the surname of her husband. According to the judgement of Lord Mountbatten of Burma, the House of Windsor ceased to exist when the newly crowned Queen married his nephew, and any issue from the marriage would be from the House of Mountbatten. Upon learning of this, Queen Mary, the consort of King George V, made Prime Minister Winston Churchill aware of the dilemma. Agreeing that the name of the Royal House should not be changed, the Prime Minister then advised The Queen that she should issue a proclamation stating that her House and issue would remain as the Royal House of Windsor.

Her Majesty's Proclamation on 9th April 1952 stated that it was her "Will and Pleasure that I and My children shall be styled and known as the House and Family of Windsor, and that My descendants, other than female descendants who marry and their descendants, shall bear the name of Windsor." Eight years later, on 8th February 1960, The Queen confirmed that she and those of issue from her and Prince Philip would continue to be styled as House of Windsor, as would any agnatic descendants who enjoy the style of "Royal Highness" whilst the title of Prince or Princess and

that her agnatic descendants who do not bare the title Prince or Princess would be styled Mountbatten-Windsor in honour of her husband, Prince Philip. As a Royal Proclamation does not have statutory authority within the United Kingdom, any future monarch can change the name of the Royal House at will through a similar proclamation like that of King George V and his granddaughter, Queen Elizabeth II.

Windsor Castle.
Photo: Thomas Mace-Archer-Mills.

By appointment to
Her Majesty The Queen
Manufacturers of ANGOSTURA® aromatic bitters
ANGOSTURA® Ltd
Trinidad, West Indies

Their Majesties' Mixers

Sponsored by ANGOSTURA® aromatic bitters:

For almost 200 years, **ANGOSTURA®** aromatic bitters, created by J.G.B Siegert, has been the key ingredient in many cocktails and cuisine delights. Beginning as a medicinal product to cure the malady of the stomach, this mixture of herbs and spices has evolved into a product that is now the talk of the town and one that can be seen in the best of bars and restaurants around the world.

ANGOSTURA® aromatic bitters has been famous since 1824 and holds the Royal Warrant to The Queen of England's household for many years. It is a staple fixture at any bar, and bartenders the world over say that it is a unique product that they would not do without in their field of work. Distilled in the island of Trinidad, using the same secret recipe since inception, it is versatile beyond belief. It has been said to flavour and enhance anything that it is added to.

The experts say that it "matures a Manhattan", "makes the Old Fashioned" and "mellows the diverse taste of rum drinks". It can round a beer, cause vodka to flower and smooth a whiskey sour. And it works wonders for non-alcoholic drinks as well. The mere presence of **ANGOSTURA®** aromatic bitters is an indication of sophistication.

To truly see the versatility of the product that 'flavours the world', one needs to try the many ways in which it can be used. Some like it in tea and coffee, some in gravies and soups. It has also become popular in fresh fruit salads and on top of vanilla and coconut ice cream.

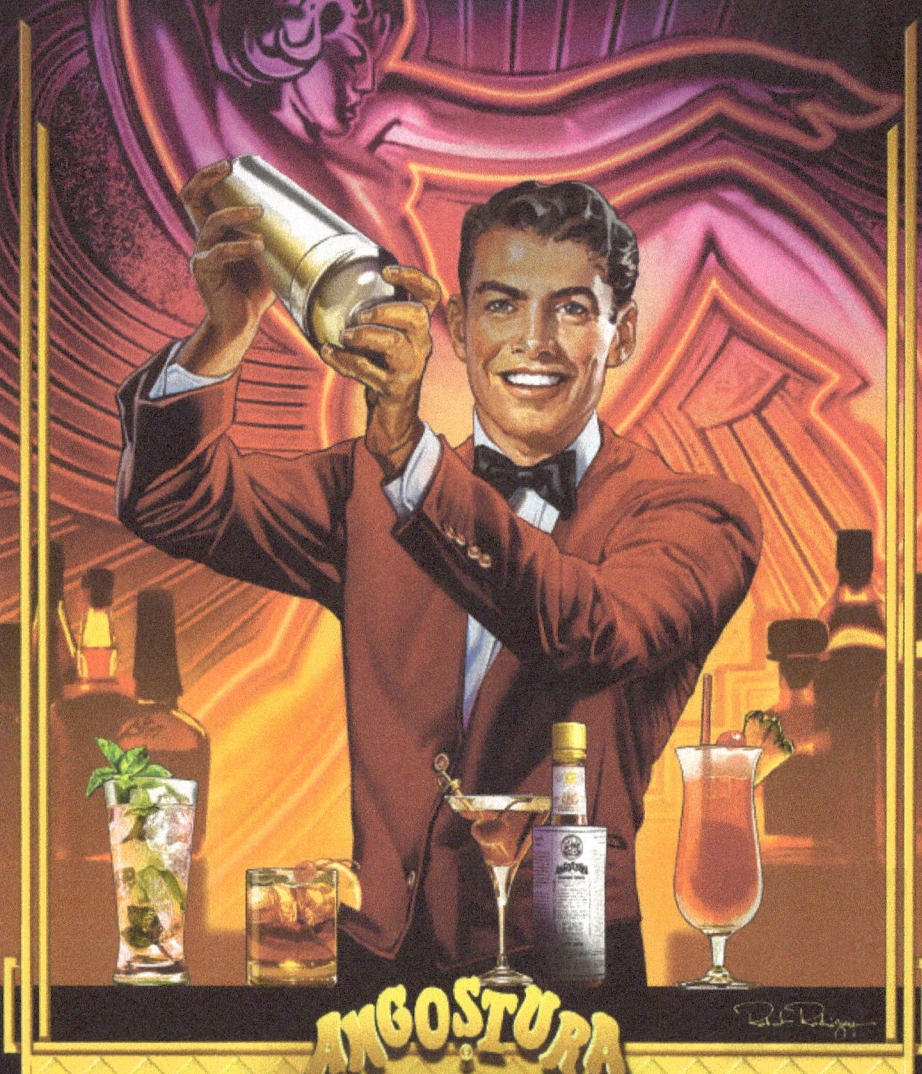

ANGOSTURA
aromatic bitters

The story of **ANGOSTURA**® aromatic bitters is a journey through time. In the 1870s, Dr. Siegert's three sons migrated to Trinidad, among them Don Carlos Siegert, who pioneered the brand, establishing **ANGOSTURA**® aromatic bitters as an integral ingredient in cocktails and in food. The rest, as they say, is history. **ANGOSTURA**® aromatic bitters is today a staple for bartenders and cocktail enthusiasts, professional and home cooks alike, bounded only by the creativity and imaginations of those who use it.

Bitters create wonderful layers of flavour, and bring balance to drink and food recipes in just a few magical dashes. **ANGOSTURA**® aromatic bitters is classic and impressively versatile, and is a must-have ingredient in bars and kitchens. In existence since 1824, their expert blending knowledge has led to the creation of **ANGOSTURA**® orange bitters and Amaro di **ANGOSTURA**®. These innovations continue to drive the creativity and imaginations of bartenders and chefs around the world. A bottle of **ANGOSTURA**® aromatic bitters in the kitchen is a hallmark of a good cook. It works by enhancing the flavour of other ingredients in food and drink preparations – it brings out the best flavours without masking their personality and adds a unique but subtle flavour of its own. The world's best chefs view this exotic and versatile bitters as a culinary essential. Experiment with **ANGOSTURA**® orange bitters in jams, jellies and desserts, including ice cream and fudge. Perfect paired with chocolate! This bitters works well in sauces and is particularly delicious complement to seafood dishes.

Did you know?

- **ANGOSTURA**® aromatic bitters is not bitter. "Bitters" is simply the generic category for products made from tropical herbs and spices.
- It adds a unique but subtle flavour of its own. The flavour is impossible to describe; you have to experience it.
- **ANGOSTURA**® aromatic bitters marries and enhances the flavours of the other ingredients in food and drink preparation. It brings out the 'best' in them. It does not mask the other flavours.
- It tempers the acidity of citrus ingredients. This is particularly important for those who are acid sensitive.
- The label of every bottle still bears a facsimile of the signature of Dr J.G.B. Siegert.
- Chefs use it to marinade poultry and add flavour to fish, and even dash it atop a delicious dessert fit for a king.

A bottle of **ANGOSTURA**® aromatic bitters in the kitchen is the hallmark of a good cook and at the bar, one of a true connoisseur.

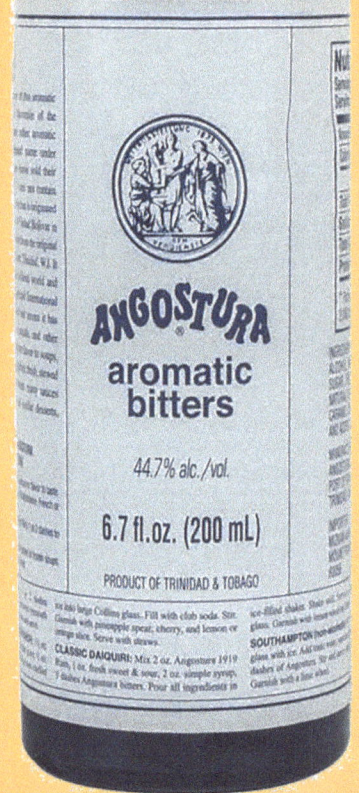

Orange Bitters

Angostura®, the world's leader in aromatic bitters, had employed all of its considerable blending expertise to create this exquisite orange bitters. Citrus from tropical oranges have been perfectly combined with exotic spices to create a rich and bold orange bitters. Softly scented with geranium, ANGOSTURA® orange bitters offers a dry, intense flavour, with spicy notes and a finish of complex bitter oranges.

ANGOSTURA® orange bitters is the essential ingredient for those who embrace artistry in cocktail construction. Its complex layered notes, anchored by a balanced orange zest flavour, works incredibly well with vodka, gin and whisky and add real depth of flavour to rum cocktails. It is the indispensable ingredient in the classic dry Martini.

ANGOSTURA® aromatic bitters is not bitter when added to food and drink – bitters is simply the category for products made from gentian aromatic herbs and spices. An essential ingredient, **ANGOSTURA**® bitters has over 190 years of well-preserved tradition and expertise behind its name. Start dashing! A world of flavour and enjoyment awaits.

Broiled Lemon-Garlic Shrimp

Ingredients

- ⅓ cup olive oil
- grated peel of one large lemon
- ¼ cup lemon juice
- ¼ cup chopped coriander or Italian parsley
- 1 tbsp ANGOSTURA® aromatic bitters
- 2 cloves garlic, crushed
- 1 tsp salt (or to taste)
- ½ tsp hot pepper sauce
- 1 kilo (approx 2lb) large shrimp with tails on, approx. 21/25 size (jumbo sized)
- 8 (10-inch) skewers
- lemon slices, to serve (optional)

Makes 8 servings (5 shrimps each)

Method

In a non-metallic bowl, combine ingredients except shrimp and skewers; stir well. Peel and de-vein shrimp, leaving tails on. Add to marinade and stir to coat. Cover and refrigerate for 1 to 1 ½ hours. Heat broiler. Top a large sheet tray with a baking rack. Drain shrimp and thread on skewers; place skewers on rack. Broil for 3-5 minutes or until cooked through. Serve with lemon slices, if desired.

Recipe by Rita Held

Pulled Pork Sliders with Angostura Bitters

Ingredients

Angostura® Chili Rub
- 2 tbsp ANGOSTURA® aromatic bitters
- 2 tbsp chili powder*
- 1 tsp salt
- 3 - 3 ½ lbs (1.5 kilos) boneless pork shoulder roast*
- 1 tbsp cooking oil (corn, safflower or canola)

ANGOSTURA® Sauce
- 1 medium can unseasoned tomato sauce or two 8 oz cans*
- ½ cup packed dark brown sugar
- 2 tbsp cider vinegar
- 1 tbsp ANGOSTURA® aromatic bitters
- 1 tbsp chili powder
- 3 large cloves garlic, chopped
- 1 - 2 tbsp cornstarch, if needed, for slow-cooker sauce*

Method

Hob method. Stir together ANGOSTURA® aromatic bitters, chili powder and salt; let stand 10 minutes. Cut meat across the grain into 1½ to 2" (2-3 cm) thick slices; trim excess fat. If needed, cut into chunks to remove some of the fat. Rub meat with chili mixture. Heat oil in a large pot or 9-10" wide (24 cm), high-sided sauté pan with lid. Add meat and brown on both sides, about 15 minutes total. Remove meat to a plate; keep warm. (While meat browns, combine sauce ingredients.)

ANGOSTURA® Sauce

Combine tomato sauce and remaining ingredients except cornstarch; stir well. Pour into hot, empty pan. Simmer 5 minutes, stirring and scraping bottom of pan. Return meat to pan; spoon sauce over meat. Cover and cook on low heat for 1 hour 15 minutes, rearranging meat halfway through. Transfer meat to a plate; cover with foil to keep warm.

To thicken sauce if desired, let sauce cool in pan for 5 minutes, then whisk in cornstarch. Bring to a boil; continue to cook and whisk until slightly thickened. To serve, pull meat apart with a fork or your fingers. Serve warm on buns, drizzled with sauce.

Makes 7-8 cups pulled pork with 1½ cups sauce (for approx 14 small sandwiches)

Slow cooker method - total cook time about 4½ hours

Follow stove top directions for meat and sauce.

Place browned meat in a 5-6 quart slow-cooker. After sauce has simmered for 5 minutes in the same pan used to brown the meat, add sauce to slow cooker. Cover and cook on low for 4 hours (or high for 2 hours).

Turn off cooker and remove meat to a plate or cutting board; keep warm. Whisk 1 tablespoon cornstarch into hot sauce in slow cooker. Continue to whisk until sauce has thickened. Add an additional tbsp cornstarch, if desired.

Makes 2+ cups sauce.

Kitchen Notes:

- Chili powder brands vary. If you like it spicy, use a brand that has cayenne pepper or ground chipotle chilis.

- Boneless pork shoulder roast is also known as Boston butt roast.

- Brands of tomato sauce vary in consistency. If the cooked sauce seems thick enough, do not use cornstarch. Cornstarch will be needed for the slow cooker, however.

- Nutrition information per serving (14) without buns, using 3-1/2 lbs pork: 334.9 calories, 21.7g fat (7.3g sat fat), 81 mg chol, 20.2g protein, 12.2g carbs, 430mg sodium, 1.1g fibre.

ANGOSTURA® aromatic bitters adds rich flavour to pulled pork. Similar to our Roast Beef & Gravy recipe, bitters is rubbed on the meat and added to the sauce.

Recipe by Rita Held

Fiesta Meatballs with Ancho Dipping Sauce

Mini meatballs — with a Mexican twist and ANGOSTURA® aromatic bitters — makes a tasty appetiser for entertaining. The meatballs and sauce can be made a day or two ahead. Keep refrigerated and warm up in the microwave just before serving.

Ingredients

Fiesta Meatballs
- 1¼ lb (625 g) lean ground beef
- ¼ cup dry breadcrumbs
- 1 tbsp Ancho chili powder
- ½ tsp ground cumin
- ½ tsp oregano
- ½ tsp salt
- ½ cup finely chopped onion
- 3 cloves garlic, minced
- 1 large egg
- 1 tsp ANGOSTURA® aromatic bitters or 2 tbsp ANGOSTURA® orange bitters

Ancho Dipping Sauce
- 1 medium can (8 oz) plain tomato sauce
- 1 tbsp packed brown sugar
- 1 tsp ANGOSTURA® aromatic bitters
- 1 tsp red or white wine vinegar
- 1 tsp Ancho chili powder
- ½ tsp ground cumin

Makes about 40 meatballs (approx 1" diameter) and 1 cup+ dipping sauce.

Method

Preheat oven to 400°F (200°C). Lightly grease a large sheet tray. Place ground beef in a medium bowl. In a small bowl, stir together breadcrumbs, ancho powder, cumin, oregano and salt. Stir in onion and garlic. Sprinkle over meat in two batches, cutting into meat with the side of a large spoon. Whisk together egg and ANGOSTURA® bitters. Drizzle over meat, cutting in with spoon. Form into 1" (3 cm) meatballs and place on sheet tray. Bake 16-18 minutes.

Stir together sauce ingredients and warm up in microwave. Serve with meatballs and toothpicks.

Recipe by Rita Held

Kitchen Notes:

- If you make smaller meatballs, decrease the baking time by 2-3 minutes.

- Like it extra spicy? Stir hot sauce or chipotle chili powder into the dipping sauce.

- Nutrition for two meatballs dipped in sauce: 70 calories, 3.2 g fat (1.3 g sat fat), 28 mg cholesterol, 6.4 g protein, 3.3 g carbohydrate, 58.9 mg sodium, 0.5 g fibre

www.angosturabitters.com

FUN ANGOSTURA® aromatic bitters FACTS...DID YOU KNOW?

- *Interior Designers, Take Note* - Jamie Boudreau, owner of Canon Bar in Seattle, WA, used three cases of 16 oz ANGOSTURA® aromatic bitters to stain and decorate the inside of his bar. This makes Canon Bar possibly the first bar in the world to have all its wooden furniture and fittings stained with bitters.

  Caution - ANGOSTURA® aromatic bitters stains if spilled on clothes, cloth, wood or any other surface and if left to dry, you will not be able to remove the stain.

- *Gourmet Tip* - ANGOSTURA® aromatic bitters is not bitter when added to food and drinks - bitters is simply the generic category for products made from gentian, aromatic herbs and spices.

- *Common Misconception* - ANGOSTURA® aromatic bitters does not contain Angostura trifoliata, a medicinal plant native to South America which is commonly misconstrued as being used in the brand's bitters. ANGOSTURA® aromatic bitters is, in fact, named after the capital of Venezuela's south-eastern Bolivar State, which was founded as Angostura in 1764 and renamed Ciudad Bolivar in 1846. ANGOSTURA® aromatic bitters were invented by founder Dr. Johann Siegert in the Venezuelan city in 1824 as a medicinal tincture, designed to alleviate stomach ailments during his tenure as Surgeon-General for Simón Bolívar's revolutionary troops.

THE HISTORY OF ANGOSTURA (1824-1955)

Within lies the history of a great brand, ANGOSTURA® aromatic bitters, a product that has withstood the test of time, has remained a secret recipe, has affected trade policies through its classification, and is today known as the "Taste that flavours the world".

aromatic bitters

By Appointment to
Her Majesty The Queen
Manufacturers of Angostura aromatic bitters
Angostura Ltd
Trinidad & Tobago

1824 — Dr. Siegert perfects the formula for aromatic bitters.

1875 — Bitters manufacturing moves to Port Of Spain, Trinidad

| 1903 | 1921 | 1949 | 1955 |

1903 — J.G.B Siegert & Hijos appointed purveyors of Angostura aromatic bitters to his majesty King George V.

1921 — Angostura Bitters Ltd formed as a registered company.

1949 — Trinidad Distillers Ltd is established.

1955 — The company is appointed manufacturers of Angostura aromatic bitters to Her Majesty Queen Elizabeth II.

Carlos

Alfredo

Robert

Albert

Thomas

Fernandes

Royal Brandy Drinks

*"When I am an old woman I shall wear purple,
With a red hat which doesn't go, and doesn't suit me,
And I shall spend my pension on Brandy and summer gloves
And satin sandals, and say we've no money for butter".*

Jenny Joseph (1932 - 2018), British Poet

Brandy, or "burnt wine", is a derivative of the Dutch "brandewijn" which is an alcohol (spirit) produced from the distillation of wine. Unlike its grain counterparts gin and whisky, which can be made throughout the year, brandy is an alcohol that is dependent on the seasons. The ripened fruits that are harvested must first be produced into wine, which is then distilled for the production of the alcohol from which brandy is made. In addition to fermented grapes, brandy is also produced from other fermented fruits which are referred to in French as 'eaux-de-vie'. Due in part to the ingredients used, brandy is an agricultural alcohol where its base must be ripened in order to enter the fermenting and distilling process, much like rum. Brandy can vary in alcohol content, but usually measures about 35 to 60 per cent alcohol by volume.

Brandy's origination corresponds with the growth and development of the process of distillation. Today's brandy can trace its roots to the twelfth century eventually becoming widely popularised by the fourteenth century. To make its transport easier for merchants, wine was initially distilled as a preservation method for long journeys as well as a way to lessen its tariffs which were excised by its mass. Upon arrival of the wine, the intent was to replace the water that was removed before consumption. After travelling for vast amounts of time in storage casks made of wood, it was found that "brandy" was an improvement over the original spirit being transported. Mostly known as an after-dinner drink, it was common that during the turn of the twentieth century through to the 1960s, prominent gentlemen in society when gathered, would excuse themselves to enjoy a brandy and a smoke. Brandies are typically aged like its other alcoholic counterparts in wooden casks, whilst some others are coloured with caramel colouring. There are certain labels that use both aging and colouring to produce their brandy, whilst other labels use fruit flavouring to create a distinct flavour and brand. As an agricultural alcohol whose base is primarily comprised of grapes, it is not unexpected that most brandies originate from regions of high wine production. Some of the best brandies (at present, as well as historically) happen to come from regions that produce the best wines, such as France, Spain and the far reaches of Eastern Europe, as well as the Eurasian plateau (where brandy was referred to as cognac). Different types of brandies have often tended to be specific to their location of production, therefore this identifying trait leads to certain brandy-making areas specifying the type of grape or fruit that can be used and where it can be grown.

Historically, it has been the vast cellars of the Romanov Court in Russia's Imperial Capital of St. Petersburg that have been famed for their expansive and quality cognacs, brandies and wines. This collection became legendary as much of it was lost after the collapse of the Romanov dynasty. The October Revolution of 1917 saw the grand Winter Palace stormed and once the Palace was taken, the army took a week-long hiatus so that they could imbibe large quantities of the collection whilst they pillaged the Palace for its treasures, art and fine furnishings. Though the Russian monarchy ended and its famed collection of wines, brandies and cognacs made legend by communist thugs and murders, the age of Russian brandy production was anything but dead. As Russia began to emerge from its dark days of the Revolution and head into the Soviet era, it was the Communist governments of the day that kept the production of brandy a source of pride for the people. The Soviet Union produced some of the best quality brandies which are still sought after today, especially their famous jubilee brandies of 1967, 1977 and 1987.

Brandy, for the connoisseur, is mostly drank neat or on the rocks but others may choose to mix it with additional liqueurs or mixers to create other cocktails, such as the well-known Brandy Alexander, Brandy Old Fashioned, Brandy Sour or the Sidecar. For those who choose to enjoy brandy in its pure form, they would know that when brandy is consumed at room temperature, it is usually cupped in the palm of the hand (in a special glass known as a 'brandy snifter') which slightly warms it. Some people choose to heat their brandies before consuming it. However, excessive heating of the spirit may cause the alcohol vapours to become too strong thus rendering the brandy overpowering. Contrary to popular belief, brandy fares better at a lower temperature which means that the spirit should be consumed cooled rather than heated to fully enjoy the full and smooth feel of the alcohol. Heating the brandy tends to make the alcohol thinner and less full-bodied which can create a burning sensation when consumed.

The Throne

- 1 ½ oz (40 ml) lime juice
- 1 tsp superfine sugar
- 2 measures of brandy
- 1 dash bitters
- 3 oz (85 ml) Club Soda
- crushed ice
- lime rind, to garnish

Method: It has been a while, but let me reintroduce you to our friend, the shaker. In the shaker, add the lime juice, sugar, brandy and bitters then shake and shimmy vigorously to your favourite tunes until your hands hurt from the cold. Then, in a collins glass filled with crushed ice, swizzle the ice until the glass itself is frosty cold. Once the desired frost has appeared, strain the contents of the shaker into the glass and top off with Club Soda. Garnish with a lime rind and withdraw to the garden.

FUN FACT

In 1976, Her Majesty sent her first email from an Army base.

"To what greater inspiration and counsel can we turn than to the imperishable truth to be found in this treasure house, the Bible?"
Queen Elizabeth II

The Royal Coat of Arms

- 1 measure apple brandy
- 1 measure sweet sherry
- 2 measures sparkling apple juice

Method: In an old-fashioned glass, stir in all ingredients with broken ice, give a quick swirl of the glass and serve. You know what they say, an apple a day...

FUN FACT

The Queen's first Commonwealth tour began on 24th November 1953. The tour included visits to Bermuda, Jamaica, Panama, Fiji, Tonga, New Zealand, Australia, the Cocos Islands, Ceylon, Aden, Uganda, Libya, Malta and Gibraltar. The total distance covered was 43,618 miles.

> "It is easy enough to define what the Commonwealth is not.
> Indeed this is quite a popular pastime."
> Queen Elizabeth II

The Royal Cypher

- 2 ½ oz brandy
- 1 tsp powdered sugar
- 8 mint leaves

Method: In an empty collins glass, place at the bottom of the glass the sugar, mint leaves and brandy. Follow through with filling the glass with finely-shaved ice and stir ever so gently so that the mint leaves rise to the top. You must be gentle with this process so as not to bruise the mint leaves. You may garnish with a pineapple, orange, lemon and/or a cherry; however, I prefer less fruit and more drink.

FUN FACTS

In 1986, Her Majesty became the first British monarch to visit China.

Her Majesty was the first British monarch to send her children to boarding school, to escape the ever-present media intrusion into their lives.

The Queen chooses not to wear a riding hat, and is often seen wearing only a headscarf on her head.

A Royal Peculiar

- 2 oz brandy
- ½ oz Triple Sec
- 2 ½ oz ginger ale
- mint leaves and fruit slice, to garnish

Method: Combine all the ingredients in a rocks glass filled with crushed ice. Dip a quick swizzle and garnish with mint leaves and a fruit slice of your choice, if so desired. Remember, a Royal Peculiar is a place of religious bearing so try not to consume too much… on the other hand, some of those monks certainly knew how to distil and enjoy!

FUN FACTS

In 1953, The Queen made the first Christmas Broadcast from overseas (rather than from the UK), broadcasting live from New Zealand. The first televised broadcast was aired live in 1957. The first pre-recorded broadcast took place in 1960 to allow transmission around the world.

Her Majesty has 30 godchildren.

The Queen was shot at six times during the 1981 Trooping the Colour. Luckily, the perpetrator only fired blanks.

The Royal Mews

- 2 oz brandy
- 5 oz ginger ale
- 2 dashes ANGOSTURA® bitters
- lemon spiral, to garnish

Method: In a highball glass filled with ice, pour the brandy, ginger ale and bitters, and swizzle well. The lemon spiral should be draped over the rim of the glass for proper presentation, but I tend to put mine on a friend's glass so that it does not obstruct my imbibing ability of this light and tasty cocktail. Remember, these go down quite well... so think twice before having too many. Enjoy!

FUN FACT

The Queen has made an annual Christmas Broadcast to the Commonwealth every year of her reign except in 1969. A repeat of the film 'Royal Family' was shown that year and a written message from The Queen issued.

"The upward course of a nation's history is due, in the long run, to the soundness of heart of its average men and women."
Queen Elizabeth II

A Right Royal

- 2 oz brandy
- ¼ tsp sugar syrup
- 2 dashes ANGOSTURA® bitters
- twist lemon peel, to garnish

Method: In a mixing glass, shake all ingredients well with ice until a light foam appears. Strain into a cocktail glass and garnish with a lemon peel. You may choose to serve to others, but I sometimes find that when I have more, the merrier everyone else is!

The only way to know that you have indeed enjoyed this wonderful cocktail, is to make sure that the foam not only appears on the top of the drink, but on the top of your lip as well! Take a selfie!

FUN FACT

The Queen undertook her first State Visit as Princess Elizabeth, with King George VI and Queen Elizabeth, to South Africa from February to May 1947. The tour included Rhodesia and Bechuanaland, Swaziland and Basutoland. The Princess celebrated her 21st birthday in Cape Town, South Africa where she made a speech dedicating her life in service to the people of the Commonwealth.

The Queen's Summer Solstice Smash

- ½ yellow nectarine
- 1 lemon wedge
- 1 tangerine wedge
- 4 chocolate mint leaves
- ½ oz peach liqueur
- ½ oz cognac
- ½ oz simple syrup

Method: Turning to our trusty friend, the shaker, muddle the nectarine, lemon and tangerine at the bottom of the shaker. Take a moment to let the fruits marry whilst going ahead and bruising the mint leaves to ensure a full mint flavour will be present. If your fingers smell minty, you have done this properly. Once the fruit has had time to breathe, add the ice, liqueur, simple syrup, cognac and mint to the mixture and that's right, you guessed it… shake away until frosty cold. Continue to strain the ingredients into an old-fashioned glass filled with crushed ice. After a couple of these, you will become eclipsed!

FUN FACT

Her Majesty sent a message of congratulations to the Apollo 11 astronauts for the first moon landing on 21st July 1969. The message was microfilmed and deposited on the moon in a metal container.

"They are not royal. They just happen to have me as their aunt."
Queen Elizabeth II

"I myself prefer my New Zealand eggs for breakfast."
Queen Elizabeth II

Stone of Scone (Stane o Scuin) Punch

- ¾ oz whisky
- ¾ oz brandy
- ¾ oz Bénédictine Liqueur
- juice of ½ orange
- juice of ½ lemon
- tonic water
- orange and lemon slice, to garnish

Method: Rinse out that shaker and here we go again. Shake the aforementioned ingredients together with ice until cold. Strain the mixture over shaved ice into a Collins glass and top up with tonic water then swizzle the drink for a few seconds – not more than 5. You may garnish with an orange and lemon slice and continue to repeat these steps in 5-10 minutes. One too many of these will surely see you fall right off your throne!

FUN FACTS

The Stone of Scone is also known as the Stone of Destiny, and often referred to in England as the Coronation Stone. The stone was used for centuries in the coronation of Scottish monarchs and later the monarchs of England and eventually the kingdom of Great Britain.

Her Majesty's first State Visit as Queen was technically to Kenya, as King George VI died when she was there on tour. She ascended the throne at Tree Top Villas where she took the name Elizabeth II as Queen.

The Queen has nine Royal Thrones: one in the House of Lords, two in Westminster Abbey and six in Buckingham Palace.

The Throne Room - Buckingham Palace.

The Olympic Queen

- 1 measure brandy
- 1 measure Triple Sec
- 1 measure orange juice
- orange peel, to garnish

Method: Shake, shake, shake, shake, shake, shake, shake your booty! In that ice-filled friendly shaker, froth the ingredients until the shaker becomes frosty cold. Strain into an already chilled Martini or cocktail glass and garnish with an orange peel. Remember, one is never enough, so invest in a larger shaker to limit physical fatigue.

FUN FACTS

During the 2012 London Olympics, Her Majesty made her film debut in 'Happy and Glorious', where she starred opposite James Bond (007) as a part of the opening Olympic ceremony. Her Majesty was seen to jump from a helicopter above the Olympic Stadium before appearing in the stadium and declaring the games open.

Always making history, 1982 was no exception when Pope John Paul II visited Britain. He was the first Pope to do so for 450 years, in which The Queen, Titular Head of the Church of England, received him at Buckingham Palace.

It is said that Her Majesty keeps a yellow rubber duck and an inflatable crown in her bath.

From the 2012 Olympic film short, "Happy & Glorious", starring Daniel Craig as James Bond and Her Majesty, Queen Elizabeth II as herself.

Royal Champagne Drinks

"My only regret in life is that I did not drink more champagne."

John Maynard Keynes (1883 - 1946), English Economist

Yes, it is French but it was an Englishman who invented and perfected the method by which champagne is now known. Despite English advancements in the methods of creating champagne and though it be little known to the masses, 'Brut' champagne was intentionally created for the British market in 1846 by Perrier-Jouët. In diversifying his production of champagne (in which sweet champagne was the style of the day), Perrier-Jouët on purpose did not sweeten the beverage before its transport to England, thus creating the champagne which is most often drank today. Being ever so tasty, some call it 'sparkling wine' but in the true spirit of this alcohol 'champagne' is ever so fitting as it is a reflection of the lustre associated with symbols of luxury and the elite as the French intended.

It was not until the mid nineteenth century that champagne became one of the most popular beverages in the world. It began in the mid 1800s and truly exploded during the Bell Époque at the end of the century. In fact, champagne greatly rose in popularity and exportation from as many as 20 million bottles being produced in 1850 as opposed to the marginal 300,000 bottles produced in 1800. Today, an average of 330 million bottles of champagne is produced annually, proving that champagne has continued its trend as being a popular beverage through the years.

Champagne became popular due to its close association with the anointment of the kings of France. The crowned heads of Europe and their courts helped promote this crisp refreshing drink as the beverage most closely associated with luxury and power. Champagne by definition is "a sparkling wine produced by inducing 'in-bottle secondary fermentation'" of the wine to effect carbonation. The term "champagne" is used to refer to wine produced using this method exclusively within the Champagne region of France, from which it takes its name. The top champagne houses have always highlighted the heritage and historical royal association of champagne to promote their product as exclusive. A luxury drink for festive and special occasions.

Champagne is created from different blends of Pinot Noir, Pinot Gris, Chardonnay and Pinot Meunier grapes. There are very strict rules, bound through international European Union treaties as well as French national law, governing the production of champagne. Only grapes grown in the specifically designated areas of the Champagne region, known as appellation, can be used for the production of champagne. Even the term "champagne" can only be used by those varieties of wine products that come from there. The American government maintains regulations that allow its own producers of 'sparkling wine' to use the term champagne under very special circumstances.

Champagne is usually served in its own glass known as a champagne flute, which is identified by its long tall hollow stem and narrow bowl of thin sides. Champagne is best served cold; an ideal serving temperature should be 7 - 9°C (45 - 48°F). Champagne should always be chilled appropriately before serving. Therefore, if it's not been chilled, pop it into a bath of ice and water in a champagne bucket.

Though the French are credited with the development of champagne, it was the Romans who planted the vast vineyards in the north-east area of France where grape cultivation for the making of wine dates to around the fifth century. Since medieval times, churches and monasteries have owned the vast majority of vineyards to make wines for the Holy Eucharist. The monks were responsible for the production of such alcohol. As the French kings were traditionally anointed in Rheims, it was the local wines from the Champagne region which were served as part of the coronation festivities, hence advancing the reputation of the region as the place for posh tipple.

The first account of the creation of a sparkling wine (a Blanquette de Limoux) is credited to the Benedictine Monks of the Abbey of Saint-Hilaire near Carcassonne in 1531. However, the 1670s saw another Benedictine monk, Dom Pérignon, refining the technique as cellar master in the valley of Hautvillers. Often mistakenly called the "Father of champagne", it was Dom Pérignon who perfected the grape blending, creating clear white wines and introducing thicker bottles and corks instead of wood - using hemp strings soaked in oil to hold the corks in place. However, he was only improving on the original work of an English scientist called Christopher Merret who, in 1662, eight years before Dom Pérignon's rise to fame, formulated the second fermentation of the wine by adding sugar to the mixture. Merret submitted written documentation of his experiments to The Royal Society which detail his findings and the advancement of the beverage itself with the Champagne Method or "Méthode Champenoise". Méthode Champenoise is the secondary fermentation after the still wine has fermented in the vats. Yeast and sugar are added to the wine which is then bottled and capped, not corked. The wine mixture is allowed to ferment for a period of weeks, or sometimes longer. During this process, the yeast reacts with the sugar which traps carbon dioxide in the bottle.

Once this second fermentation and the resting period are both complete, any yeast and remaining sediment must be removed from the bottle. The cellar team then position the precious bottles onto a 'riddling rack'.

This allows the wine to be rotated, at a slow speed, from a horizontal to vertical position. This draws the sediment into the neck of the bottle for easy extraction, which is termed 'disgorgement'. Once this sediment is removed, a small amount of champagne is added to fill the space for 'topping' off the bottle. It's then corked and the wire netting called a 'muselet' is put in place to keep the contents securely contained.

FUN FACT

On 29th July 1981, Dom Pérignon was chosen for the wedding of Prince Charles and Lady Diana Spencer. The magnums of Dom Pérignon Vintage 1961 carried a special insignia created just for the ceremony.

Buckingham Palace Garden

- 1 measure vodka
- ½ measure Grand Marnier
- ½ measure of fresh lime juice
- 1 tsp Triple Sec
- champagne
- 2 dashes ANGOSTURA® bitters

Method: In a shaker, bring the vodka, Grand Marnier, Triple Sec and lime juice to a frigid froth. Pour this mixture into a large champagne flute and top gracefully with champagne. Serve with two dashes of ANGOSTURA® bitters.

FUN FACTS

In the summer of 2005, The Queen opened the first "children's trail" in the Buckingham Palace garden for the Summer Opening.

Her Majesty has a mischievous side and has been known to speak in riddles to confuse her husband, Prince Philip, when they are having a family argument.

Buckingham Gate

- 3 measures Hypnotiq Liqueur
- 3 measures champagne
- ½ measure grenadine
- strawberry, to garnish

Method: In the shaker with ice, bring the Hypnotiq and grenadine to a chilled frothy mixture. Pour ice-cold champagne into a chilled champagne flute and follow it with a slow steady pour of the Hypnotiq and grenadine mixture. Garnish with strawberry, if desired.

FUN FACT

Her Majesty's official wedding cake was made by McVitie and Price Ltd using ingredients given as a wedding gift by Australian Girl Guides.

"It is as Queen of Canada that I am here. Queen of Canada and all Canadians, not just one or two ancestral strains."
Queen Elizabeth II

"I sometimes sense the world is changing almost too fast for its inhabitants, at least for us older ones."
Queen Elizabeth II

Kensington Palace

- 1 measure melon liqueur
- ⅓ measure Sweet and Sour Mix
- champagne
- fresh melon slices, to garnish

Method: In a tall, chilled champagne flute, pour the melon liqueur and the Sweet and Sour Mix into the flute, top with champagne and garnish with fresh melon slices.

FUN FACT

The Queen's real birthday is on 21st April, but is officially celebrated on the second Saturday of June. The reason for an official birthday in June actually dates back to the early 1800s where the birthday of the sovereign was moved to the early summer to take advantage of the better weather. Her Majesty celebrates her actual birthday in a low-key fashion; however, her official birthday is a different matter, celebrated with parades, massed bands and a Royal Air Force flyover. Her Majesty presides over Trooping the Colour and presents new colours to a chosen regiment. She also spends time with her family on the balcony of Buckingham Palace, greeting the crowds who have come to give their best wishes. The day's events are concluded with a 21-gun salute in Green Park along with a coloured flight of red, white and blue by the Red Arrows.

The Princess Margaret

- 3 generous measures champagne
- 1 measure gold rum
- 1 measure orange juice (with pulp)
- ½ measure lemon juice
- ¼ measure grenadine syrup
- lemon and orange peel, to garnish

Method: Using your shaker filled with ice, shake all of the ingredients, except the champagne, until the shaker is riddled with frost. Strain the mixture into a large white wine glass and top off with champagne. Serve with a lemon and orange peel as garnish.

FUN FACT

Princess Margaret was born on 21st August 1930 in Glamis, the family seat of her mother's family. She was the first member of the British Royal Family to be born in Scotland for over 300 years.

"It's a question of one maturing into something, that one's not used to doing."
- On becoming Queen.
Queen Elizabeth II

The Garter Star

- 1 sugar cube
- ANGOSTURA® bitters
- champagne, chilled
- sparkling wine
- lemon twist, to garnish

Method: Soak the sugar cube with a couple of good splashes of ANGOSTURA® bitters and place in the bottom of a large champagne flute. Fill slowly with sparkling wine. Garnish with a lemon twist.

FUN FACTS

The Most Noble Order of the Garter is the highest and most exclusive order of knighthood in Britain. Traditionally, there are only 24 knights as full members at any one time, including the reigning monarch and the Prince of Wales.

The order's annual gathering is held at Saint George's Chapel at Windsor Castle, with its magnificent procession of members and retainers in full regalia. It maintains the traditions of pomp and pageantry for which the Middle Ages are rightly famous.

"These wretched babies don't come until they are ready."
Queen Elizabeth II

The RVO
(Royal Victorian Order)

- 1 measure tequila, well-chilled
- lime juice
- 1 measure Triple Sec, well-chilled
- salt
- champagne

Method: Prepare a white wine glass by rimming the lip of the glass with lime juice and dipping the glass in salt to create a crust. Continue by pouring in tequila and Triple Sec and stir gently. Top off with champagne.

FUN FACTS

Her Majesty is the first member of the British Royal Family to ever be awarded a gold disc from the recording industry. The 'Party at the Palace' CD, produced by EMI, sold 100,000 copies within the first week of release.

Her Majesty is not terribly fond of Buckingham Palace and often resides at Windsor Castle on weekends, holidays and Easter Court. Windsor is where Her Majesty considers home.

The Order of the Bath

- 1 sugar cube
- 2-3 dashes ANGOSTURA® bitters
- champagne
- 1 measure brandy
- orange slice, to garnish
- maraschino cherry, to garnish

Method: Place the sugar cube in the bottom of a champagne flute. Use the dashes of ANGOSTURA® bitters to saturate the sugar cube. Add the brandy. Fill with champagne. Garnish with the orange slice and cherry. This liquid refreshment is so delightful, one could just bathe in it! No need for a glass, just a straw!

FUN FACTS

In 1997, The Queen launched Buckingham Palace's first official website.

Her Majesty is fluent in French and often uses the language to speak with foreign Heads of State, and therefore a translator is not required.

The OBE
(Order of the British Empire)

- 1 measure gin
- 1 measure melon liqueur
- ½ measure Limoncello
- 1 measure of mango juice
- champagne

Method: Prepare an already chilled Martini glass by rimming the lip with mango juice and dipping into granulated sugar to create a sweet crust. Using our shaker, shake together the gin, melon liqueur, Limoncello and mango juice until frothy cold and frosty. Pour into the frosted glass and top with champagne.

FUN FACT

In June 2002, as part of her Golden Jubilee celebrations, The Queen hosted the first ever public concerts in her private garden at Buckingham Palace. The Queen attended both the classical and pop concerts. The 'Party at the Palace' pop concert was one of the most watched pop concerts in history, attracting around 200 million viewers all over the world.

"For me, heaven is likely to be a bit of a come-down."
Queen Elizabeth II

Golden State Coach

- champagne, generous serving
- 1 measure brandy

Method: Simply pour the brandy and champagne into a champagne flute at the same time, letting the ingredients marry, and serve.

FUN FACTS

The Gold State Coach was built for George III in 1762. It is so heavy, almost four tons, that it needs eight horses to pull it. There are three cherubs on the centre of the roof which represent the guardian spirits of England, Scotland and Ireland. They support the Sceptre, the Sword of State and the Ensign of Knighthood in their hands. It has carried every monarch to their coronation since 1821.

On the morning of her wedding, Her Majesty's bouquet was lost by a footman and her tiara snapped in two as it was being put on her head.

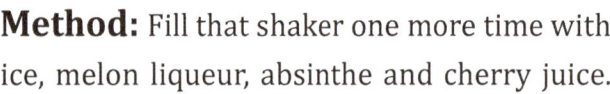

- 4 measures champagne
- 3 measures melon liqueur
- 3 measures absinthe
- 2 dashes cherry juice
- slice honey dew melon, to garnish

Method: Fill that shaker one more time with ice, melon liqueur, absinthe and cherry juice. Shake your shimmy and shaker like it is the last dance of the evening and bring the mixture to a frigid froth. Pour the contents from the shaker into an already-chilled tall champagne flute and gently top off with champagne. Garnish with a slice of honeydew melon and retire to the library, but not before leaving a note that you will clean up in the morning. Enjoy!

FUN FACT

The Queen and The Duke of Edinburgh were married on 20th November 1947 in Westminster Abbey. The Queen's wedding dress was designed by Sir Norman Hartnell (who was also the designer of her Coronation dress). It was woven at Winterthur Silks Limited, Dunfermline, in the Canmore factory using silk that had come from Chinese silkworms at Lullingstone Castle.

"I think everybody really will concede that on this, of all days, I should begin my speech with the words 'My husband and I.'"
Queen Elizabeth II, speaking at Guildhall, London on her 25th wedding anniversary.

Empress of India

- 1 sugar cube
- ½ measure Grand Marnier
- ½ measure blue Curaçao
- champagne

Method: In a champagne saucer, dissolve the cube of sugar with Grand Marnier and blue Curaçao. Top with cold dry champagne.

FUN FACTS

Her Majesty has mastered the art of travel and every mode of transportation there is. She has travelled by horse, carriage, train, plane, boat, subway, tram, trolley and even has her own fleet of horses, carriages and custom-built chauffeured Rolls Royces and Bentleys. Until 1997, she had her own private yacht named "Britannia".

Her Majesty is not solely driven around; she sometimes opts to drive herself to and from events on the royal estates.

The Queen does not enjoy Champagne. During toasts she often touches a glass to her lips without drinking it.

The Buckingham Bellini
(Sponsored by Spot White Snooker Halls)

The after hours set at Newcastle's unique leisure venue, Spot White, have joined in with the year's celebrations by enjoying a specially crafted cocktail in honour of Her Majesty The Queen, appropriately named 'The Buckingham Bellini'.

Created by owner Adam Lee Goldstone, this regally named drink is created with Chafor Estate Vintage Cuvee (one of the best vintage sparkling wines from Buckinghamshire and nearest to Windsor itself), peach puree and the addition of unique, Royal blue, edible glitter to denote the Blue Sapphire Jubilee of Her Majesty.

This wonderful celebratory cocktail is adaptable to every Royal occasion, as there are a variety of different colours of edible glitter to celebrate the many Royal milestones our longest-serving monarch has enjoyed.

In a long champagne flute, combine the following:

- 25 ml Funkin White Peach Purée
- Add a nip of edible blue glitter into the peach puree
- 200 ml Chafor Estate Vintage Cuvee sparkling wine

Method: Serve in the same long flute with no garnish. The taste of this sparkling wine is prominent and is perfectly complimented with this fragrant peach purée to create a wonderfully regal flavour. A simple way to enjoy a vast and intricate career of Royal accomplishments.

14-18 Stowell Street,
Newcastle upon Tyne, NE1 4XQ
www.spotwhite.com

HRH Prince William, The Duke of Cambridge.
Photo: Thomas Mace-Archer-Mills.

The Diamond Fizz

- 2 measures gin
- juice of 1 ½ lemon
- 1 tsp powdered sugar
- champagne, chilled

Method: It should come as no surprise that we will be shaking gin, lemon juice and powdered sugar in a shaker with ice, which must be shaken until cold. Strain the mixture into a highball glass over two ice cubes. Continue by topping off with chilled champagne, give a quick swizzle and serve.

FUN FACT

Her Majesty has access to the world's largest collection of crown jewels but it is her private collection which is the most awe-inspiring. The Queen has inherited some of the most beautiful jewels in the world, but has also been presented with and commissioned other pieces as well. Her Majesty owns the largest pink diamond in the world as well as a necklace with matching earrings of large square-cut aquamarines and diamonds, which were a gift from Brazil.

"We are not amused."
Queen Elizabeth II

Royal Gin Drinks

"I have taken more out of alcohol than alcohol has taken out of me."

Sir Winston Churchill (1874 - 1965), British Politician, Statesman and Prime Minister

Gin is a much-loved drink of not only the British people, but their Royal Family. Closely related to the continental genever or "Dutch Courage", these similar alcohols are clear in nature and infused with juniper berries and an assorted bouquet of herbs and spices. It is composed mainly from rye or wheat due their durability long after the growing season is over. Gin is naturally light-bodied and refreshing whereas genever is comprised of a mixture of wheat, corn, rye and malted barley which makes for a heartier alcohol similar in part to a stronger and more boldly-flavoured malt whisky. As the distillation is the deciding factor to the potency and flavour of the gin, it is the assortment of the ingredients such as juniper and other additives consisting of, but not limited to, anise, angelica root, cinnamon, orange peel, coriander and cassia bark, to name a few which contribute to this. Initially distilled in column stills, it is the clean process of distillation which sees very little additives of congers and flavouring agents to the mixture of gin which results in a distinct proof and flavour of the alcohol. However, each distillery has their own distinct recipe for the creation of this most refreshing and lighter of spirits.

The quality of gin is often related to its unique number of distillations, which is directly accredited to the final process of distilling in which high-quality gins are distilled and re-distilled several times.

It is during the final process of this unique art of spirit making where distilling is suspended for certain amounts of time that allows the gin (alcohol) vapours to proceed through a calculated and specialised motion. This component of distilling allows the alcohol to absorb the flavour of the oils and compounds of the specially blended bouquet of juniper berries and other elements on its short journey to the distillery condenser which flavours this world-class spirit to a very distinct flavour and complex composition.

Gin has a varied degree of complexity and composition, in which this fine spirit is widely categorised through different recipes and distilling processes. Types of gin include Plymouth Gin, Old Tom Gin and genever, or Holland Gin, which is the Dutch style of this famed spirit. London Dry Gin is the most popular and highly demanded English recipe not only in Britain but our former colonies, including America and, oddly enough, Spain. It is known to be light on the palate and popular for mixing. Britain produces mostly dry gin, primarily from the column still form of distilling, in which our gins tend to be of high proof (90° or 45% ABV) with a very distinct bouquet composed of citrus from the use of dried lemon and Scville orange peels. Spain produces a substantial amount of gin in the London dry style which is true to the column still form of distilling.

The production of gin can be traced to the mid to late sixteenth century in Italy, however the first documented and proven date for the distillation of this spirit dates from the early seventeenth-century Holland. Holland had originally produced gin as a medicine which was sold in pharmacies to treat stomach complaints, gout and gallstones. Due in part to its strong and overbearing taste, the Dutch began to flavour the "medicine" with juniper, which had a soothing quality along with medicinal properties of its own. In addition to its ability to aide in medical remedy, British troops were regularly issued "Dutch Courage" during the Thirty Years' War to help raise their core body temperature during the long campaigns they would endure in cold and damp Dutch weather.

Gordon's. It's how the Brr-rr-r-itish keep their gin up!

Brr-rr-r!

Take a tip from the cool-headed English. Fight the swelter of summer with icy smooth, crackling dry Gordon's. (After all, it's how they fought the vivid sun in India for all those many years!) Mr. Gordon's brilliant formula has kept Gordon-ites in the cold for 200 summers. No wonder it's the biggest seller in England, America, the rest of the well-refreshed world. It's a tonic. Or a Collins. Or a Martini. Or a Sour. Or a…

PRODUCT OF U.S.A. 100% NEUTRAL SPIRITS DISTILLED FROM GRAIN. 90 PROOF. GORDON'S DRY GIN CO., LTD., LINDEN, N.J.

As Holland and England share similar weather, the troops familiar with this spirit began to send and bring it to England, where it was often sold in pharmacies. Though it was originally intended for medical purposes, the distillation of such a spirit was beginning to take place on a small scale, which would become increasingly larger and less regulated which would lead to questionable distilling practices and methods. However, such issues were overlooked by the poor who had a strong thirst for this new spirit.

The origins of the rise and popular use of gin in Britain, despite the Royal status granted to companies of an alcoholic nature granted by previous monarchs, can be traced back directly to Their Majesties William and Mary of Orange. Upon assuming the highly coveted throne of England after the Glorious Revolution in 1689, King William and Queen Mary (Protestant Sovereigns) set forth a series of laws and the levy of taxes to hinder the importation of wines and spirits from Catholic nations, most importantly brandy from France. In knowing a substitute for the less available spirits would be needed, The King encouraged spirits to be made from readily available and local products such as grains of wheat and rye, whilst reducing and eventually eliminating taxes and fees on replacement spirits, such as gin. Such acts by and the creation of statutes surrounding spirits and the monarch, encouraged the distillation process of English spirits by English people.

Under the new legislation championed by King William and Queen Mary, the public were allowed to distil spirits on their own accord simply by declaring their intent to do so after a ten-day grace period from the time of expressed intent. This was an easy way for private homes and individuals to spend less on the purchase of quality gin and acquire the tools necessary to distil it within their own premises. Low-grade home-made gin was often at times of poor quality and lacked the professional tastes afforded to professionally and properly distilled gins. As gin was growing in popularity and readily available, it was sometimes included in the wages of paid workers which further helped drive up the daily volume of gin sold in England. Eventually the sheer amount of product on the market drove down the market price, which made gin less expensive to imbibe than ale, beer and wine.

Gin has remained popular and at the forefront of British spirit consumption throughout the centuries not only at home, but abroad. During the days when the sun never set on the British Empire, never did it cast a shadow on the vats of gin that accompanied our travels. Exporting to and eventually distilling in every corner of the globe that we explored, gin was the preferred drink of choice. Though the Caribbean saw a sharp rise in rum consumption and exportation, gin was the steadfast friend of the colonies and eventually the Empire. As gin consumption soared and the realisation that taxes levied on this spirit could generate much needed revenue, an excise license of £20 (£2,522.00) was introduced for retailers of the spirit in 1729. In addition to this license, a further duty of two shillings (ten pence) per gallon (4.4561 litres) was also introduced.

Despite the slowing growth and further harm caused to quality gin manufacturers by such levies, the consumption of poor quality home-made gin continued to increase dramatically. Over 7,000 shops in London alone were known to sell only spirits by the year 1730, with an average of one in four private houses selling their own version of gin.

The poor masses were known to imbibe gin to the point of no return. The abuse of the spirit became an epidemic which has been famously documented by both writers, politicians and artists. English painter, printmaker, pictorial satirist, social critic, and editorial cartoonist William Hogarth captured the feel of this period in time with his engraving titled 'Gin Lane', which portrays a scene of idleness, vice and misery that leads to madness and death within the drunken poorer social classes. English courtier and political writer Lord Hervey declared: "Drunkenness of the common people was universal, the whole town of London swarmed with drunken people from morning till night", whilst Scottish novelist Tobias Smollett observed: "In these dismal caverns ('strong water shops') they (the poor) lay until they recovered some of their faculties and then they had recourse to this same mischievous potion". Needless to say, the reputation of London, and England in general, was beginning to hang in the balance. Between 1730 and 1736, over 11 million gallons of gin were distilled in the City of London. This amount of distilled gin is significant, as it was well over 20 times the figures being distilled in the year 1690. Estimated figures show such an increase of distilled gin to be the equivalent of 14 gallons per adult male.

Public drunkenness was a problem which needed a solution, but how to go about it? It was during this time that Queen Caroline (the wife of King George II) acknowledged that London had a profound drinking problem indeed. As a "social reformer", Her Majesty made the decision that public drunkenness, and dependence of the people on gin, was a public issue which she wished to tackle. In 1736, a solution was launched – make gin prohibitively expensive. His Majesty's government decided to reduce the amount of gin being consumed by passing 'The Gin Act' which took effect at midnight on 29th September 1736. This act

more than doubled the cost of a retail license from £20 to £50, where the duty levied per gallon was raised from two shillings to £1. Even the smallest amount available for purchase was set at no less than two gallons, which the common people would not accept.

Within the first six years that the Gin Act was imposed, a minuscule number of only two retail distillers became licensed, whereas the production of gin continued to rise by approximately 50 per cent. Eventually, the masses united and the great 'Gin Riots' of London began. The public were not going to be restricted by such heavy and unfair levies

Queen Caroline.

which they viewed as the death of gin. If beer was not to be levied and licensed, then why should gin? The disgruntled masses took it upon themselves to widely and openly break the law. According to Lucy Worsley (Curator of Historic Royal Palaces), they drank their gin without a care in the world whilst the crowds chanted, "No Gin, No King, No Gin, No King!" To complicate matters even worse and show himself a man of the people (which was a publicity stunt to further inflame the discord between himself and his parents), Frederick, The Prince of Wales visited a tavern where he was seen to drink a glass of gin, which symbolically stated that he too liked gin and did not like his father, The King.

In 1742, His Majesty's government repealed the Gin Act, as it was widely deemed unenforceable, unpopular and fuelling the flames of public discord. However, a new policy was in the works, which included legislation drafted by invited participating distillers which would see reasonably high prices, licensed retailers responsible to supervising magistrates and reasonable excise duties on the spirit. These changes contained within 'The Gin Act of 1751' would see an increase of respectable distillers making and retailing gin to a high quality, where exemplary companies would become famous and luxurious brands that we are still familiar with today. This legislation is the basis upon which our existing legislation has been built. As further reforms were created and put into effect, the production of gin distillation became more evolved and refined, leading to the production of a delicately balanced spirit of subtle bouquets and aromas, and so began the ascent of gin into high society. A by-product of the newly enacted gin legislation saw the import and consumption of tea rise in popularity. It was touted as an invigorating non-alcoholic alternative to gin which was widely encouraged by His Majesty's government.

Throughout the remaining eighteenth century and well into the nineteenth century, gin gradually evolved, but not before its name and image would take a nationwide battering through the documentation of "Mother Gin's" effect on her children. It was a spirit often termed "Mother's Milk" and later "Mother's Ruin" simply for the fact that not only men but women too were under the spells cast over them by gin. It was these women who were so taken with gin, that their reliance on gin was much like the dependence of a babe to breast milk. Poorer women and ladies of the night, who were under the watchful eye of gin, often abandoned their logic as well as their mothering duties where the needs of their children were ignored. Other women would take to gin for unproven and undocumented medical remedies which were mere rumours. Such actions often at times caused more harm and foul rather than the desired outcome, which eventually would lead to their ruin and demise. Mother's Gin was a common phrase used to describe the effects of gin on the poor masses who became dependent upon the spirit throughout eighteenth-century Britain.

Gin undoubtedly has a past reputation, but it's presence in modern-day circles exudes class, sophistication, tradition and heritage. Throughout the nineteenth and early twentieth centuries, the classifications of gin were challenged and categorised. Unexpectedly, London Dry triumphed over all others. Following the trend set in the days of Queen Victoria, gin entered its extreme height of popularity towards the middle to end of her reign. Though categorised as a properly regulated spirit, gin was not excluded from the medical field by any means, as it was during this time that the ever-constant gin with tonic water (which contains quinine – a medicine used to treat malaria) was introduced to the tropical colonies as a way to combat and slow the spread of malaria, rather than consuming the foul-tasting and elusive bitterness of quinine alone.

Gin continued in popularity well through the reigns of Kings Edward VII and George V. The days of flappers, bowler hats and jazz saw gin consumed in great quantities with a understated sophistication lingering about. Ladies sipped their gins whilst planning their social diaries, as our men in uniform practically bathed in the hundreds of newly found drink recipes that would see gin as the main component. By the time Kings Edward VIII and George VI took their rightful place upon the British throne, the time and popularity of gin and its long relationship with the public had plateaued, paving the way for the introduction of other spirits, such as vodka and rum, to take hold. Though never forgotten and always maintained as a staple spirit amongst the Royal Family, aristocracy and those of a sophisticated nature, gin has remained at the heart of the British institution, when sipped, the legend incarnate and when thoroughly enjoyed, as it is meant to be, the timeline of our history played out in our heads.

Gin has come full circle and has once again risen in respect to its popularity with the younger generations who credit 007, James Bond, aka Daniel Craig, with his new Vesper Martini which is a mix of gin and vodka. At the time of writing, a September 2018 report from the Wine and Spirit Trade Association shows that gin is now responsible for 68% value growth within the entire UK spirits sector, and the gin industry has now broken the £2 billion barrier, with £532 million worth of UK gin exported in the last 12 months and £1.6 billion worth of domestic sales. This has doubled in value in just five years. New gins are coming to the market every day, infused with flavours, seasonal scents and spices. Gin distilleries, bars, lounges, and associations have been created and opened, each with their own specialised twist on this very British spirit.

In November 2016, the world's first gin hotel opened its doors to the public on Portobello Road, Notting Hill, London. The Gin Hotel is the first London distillery of its kind to allow guests to stay overnight.

Gins now number into the hundreds, without the expectation of them dwindling in number. However, some of the finest and most popular gins are those found distilled on the banks of the Thames in dry London fashion. Despite the rise in popularly of infused and flavoured gins, it is without doubt a common fact that the most consumed gin cocktail is the famed Martini. This mixture of only two parts gin to one part white vermouth garnished with olives, found its niche in the late nineteenth century, and has been the drink most closely associated with the fabled stories of power, luxury and grandeur. From the playboy Prince, to Gatsby, to Bond, the Martini does not leave room for misinterpretation. It is the drink of a bygone era, the drink which has made legends and the drink which defines the cool, subtle sophistication of those who are seen in its presence. Go ahead, pour one and discover the refined abilities and talents of your alter ego. Cheers!

The Gin Hotel.

"I prefer to see all England free, better than England sober."

Unknown Bishop's statement in The House of Lords.

Thomas' Jubilee Gin with a Twist

- gin
- tonic
- 1 lime
- 1 lemon

Method: My very own twist on a classic British summer staple. As I prefer not to formally measure but to judge my pouring, the above ingredients are freely used. In a short rocks glass filled with ice, pour the tonic a quarter of the way up the glass. Muddle one half of a lime and of a lemon and pour in the juices (this should bring you almost to half way up the glass; if not, add a little more tonic and juice). Pour in your gin (I count until about three or until the glass is 85 per cent full) then top off with tonic. Swizzle the cocktail until properly mixed and enjoy. You have never had better summer refreshment.

FUN FACTS

At the age of 13, Princess Elizabeth met, and was immediately smitten by, her future husband, now The Duke of Edinburgh.

Her Majesty has visited the sets of a number of popular British soap operas, including Coronation Street, EastEnders and Emmerdale.

Traditional British Gin and Tonic

"The gin and tonic has saved more Englishmen's lives, and minds, than all the doctors in the Empire."
Sir Winston Churchill

- 2 oz gin
- 5 oz tonic water
- 1 lime wedge
- 1 lemon wedge

Method: In a short rocks glass, fill with ice, pour tonic followed by gin into the glass. Follow with fruit wedge and stir with your favourite swizzle stick for a cool and refreshing cocktail. Serve and enjoy. Repeat these steps as often as desired.

FUN FACTS

Her Majesty is a long-time devotee of Hermes scarves – the ultimate status symbol scarf that's been worn by Grace Kelly and Hillary Clinton.

The Queen is the only person in Britain who can drive without a licence or a registration number on her car. She does not possess a passport.

HM Queen Elizabeth II Martini

- ½ measure dry vermouth
- 1 generous measure gin
- 1 ½ tsp Bénédictine Liqueur
- green olive, to garnish

Method: Stir all ingredients in a shaker or posh glass pitcher with ice. Strain into a cocktail glass and serve with a green olive. If preferred, shake in shaker until your hands hurt from the cold, then pour into a chilled Martini glass for a refreshing feel. Raise your full glass and proclaim: "To The Queen"- a toast to her health!

FUN FACTS

Her Majesty has given regular Tuesday evening audiences to 13 British Prime Ministers, her first Prime Minister being Winston Churchill, 1951-55.

Her Majesty is 5ft 4 inches, or 160cm, tall.

The Lord of Mann

- 2 measures gin
- juice ½ lemon
- 1 tsp powdered sugar
- 1 egg
- carbonated water

Method: In a shaker, shake all ingredients (except carbonated water) with ice and strain into a highball glass over two ice cubes. Fill with carbonated water, stir, serve and enjoy the experience which can only be expressed as a right Royal peculiar.

FUN FACT

Her Majesty The Queen is known to her people in the Isle of Man as the Lord of Mann.

"The British Constitution has always been puzzling and always will be."
Queen Elizabeth II

The Queen's Crush

- 1 measure Dubonnet Rouge Vermouth
- ½ measure gin
- 2 dashes ANGOSTURA® bitters
- 2 dashes orange Curaçao
- 1 dash Pastis liqueur

Method: Stir (or shake vigorously for a fully mixed and frothy cocktail) all ingredients in a shaker with ice. Strain into a cocktail glass over ice, serve, savour and enjoy.

FUN FACT

The Queen has sent more than 280,000 telegrams to couples in the UK and the Commonwealth celebrating their Diamond wedding (60 years) anniversary.

"The lessons from the peace process are clear; whatever life throws at us, our individual responses will be all the stronger for working together and sharing the load."
Queen Elizabeth II

The Royal Yacht Britannia

FUN FACTS

Many of The Queen's official tours were undertaken on the Royal Yacht Britannia, which was launched by Her Majesty on 16th April 1953. It was outfitted and commissioned for service on 11th January 1954.

Her Majesty decommissioned her beloved yacht on the advice of the Blair government in December 1997.

During this time, Britannia travelled more than a million miles on Royal and official duties of State.

"What were once only hopes for the future have now come to pass; it is almost exactly 13 years since the overwhelming majority of people in Ireland and Northern Ireland voted in favour of the agreement signed on Good Friday 1998, paving the way for Northern Ireland to become the exciting and inspirational place that it is today."
Queen Elizabeth II

The Court of St. James.

- 1 dash absinthe
- 1 dash grenadine
- ⅓ part vermouth
- ⅔ part dry gin
- cherry and lime slice, to garnish

Method: In a shaker filled with ice, pour all ingredients into the shaker and shake well (I prefer to stir, as shaking bruises the alcohol). Strain into a cocktail glass with ice, and garnish with a cherry and lime wheel. After several of these drinks, the lights of any room will be a reflection of Piccadilly Circus.

FUN FACTS

In 2002, at 76 years of age, The Queen was the oldest monarch to celebrate a Golden Jubilee. The youngest was James I (James VI of Scotland) at 51 years of age.

The Court of St. James' is the Royal Court of the United Kingdom. All Ambassadors and High Commissioners to the United Kingdom are formally received by the Court, and all Ambassadors and High Commissioners from the United Kingdom are formally accredited from the Court, not the United Kingdom, as they are representatives of The Crown.

Buckingham Palace.

- 1 oz dry vermouth
- 2 oz gin
- 1 tsp maraschino liqueur
- green olive, to garnish
- lemon twist, to garnish

Method: Stir all ingredients in a shaker or posh glass pitcher with ice. Strain into a cocktail glass, and serve with a green olive and lemon twist. If preferred, shake in the shaker and remember to wear your winter gloves, and then pour into a chilled Martini glass and roll out the red carpet!

FUN FACT

Queen Elizabeth II is the fortieth monarch since William the Conqueror obtained the crown of England in 1066.

> "I have been aware all the time that my peoples, spread far and wide throughout every continent and ocean in the world, were united to support me in the task to which I have now been dedicated with such solemnity."
> Queen Elizabeth II

Windsor Castle

- 1 oz gin
- 1 tbsp lemon juice
- 1 tbsp orange juice
- orange slice, to garnish

Method: Pour all ingredients in a shaker with ice and shake vigorously to make frothy. Strain into a cocktail glass, and serve with an orange slice.

FUN FACT

Her Majesty's father died in 1952 while she was on tour in Kenya. She was immediately named Queen and was asked to choose a royal name. "Of course," she replied calmly as she chose Elizabeth.

"Football's a difficult business and aren't they prima donnas? But it's a wonderful game."
Queen Elizabeth II

The Grenadier Guard

- 2 measures gin
- ½ tsp maraschino liqueur
- 2 dashes ANGOSTURA® orange bitters
- ½ tsp powdered sugar
- lemon twist, to garnish

Method: Stir (or shake vigorously for a fully mixed and frothy cocktail) all ingredients in a shaker with ice. Strain into a cocktail glass with ice, serve with a lemon twist and savour the flavour.

FUN FACT

The Queen has received over 3 million letters during her reign.

"It is a job for life, most people have a job and then they go home, and in this existence the job and the life go on together because you can't really divide it up. The boxes and the communications just keep on coming...I'm lucky I am a quick reader."
Queen Elizabeth II

The Coldstream Guard

- 1 generous measure gin
- ½ measure sweet vermouth
- ½ measure dry vermouth
- ½ measure White Crème De Cacao

Method: Stir the gin together with the vermouths and Crème De Cacao in an old-fashioned glass half-filled with ice cubes, and serve plain. I often rim the glass with sugar to enhance this already sweet treat to satisfy my sweet tooth.

FUN FACT

Since 1952, Her Majesty The Queen has conferred over 387,700 honours and awards.

> "I have behind me not only the splendid traditions and the annals of more than a thousand years but the living strength and majesty of the Commonwealth and Empire; of societies old and new; of lands and races different in history and origins but all, by God's Will, united in spirit and in aim."
> Queen Elizabeth II

The Irish Guard

- 1 generous measure dry gin
- ½ measure Pernod
- lime rind, to garnish

Method: Add the ingredients to a mixing glass filled with ice and stir well. Strain into a chilled cocktail glass and serve with a lime rind. After imbibing a few of these, the fog will certainly set in.

FUN FACT

The Queen is patron of more than 620 charities and organisations.

Buckingham Palace has 775 rooms. These include 19 State rooms, 52 Royal and guest bedrooms, 188 staff bedrooms, 92 offices and 78 bathrooms. The palace is 108 metres long across the front, 120 metres deep (including the central quadrangle) and 24 metres high. It has five floors.

"I have in sincerity, pledged myself to your service, as so many of you are pledged to mine. Throughout all my life and with all my heart I shall strive to be worthy of your trust."
Queen Elizabeth II

Queen Elizabeth II in the robes of The Most Noble Order of the Garter.
Photo: Thomas Mace-Archer-Mills.

God Save Our Gracious Queen

- 1 measure gin
- 1 measure apple juice
- 1 measure apricot nectar
- ½ tsp fresh lemon juice
- lime wheel or rind, to garnish

Method: Stir (or shake vigorously for a fully mixed and frothy cocktail) all ingredients in a shaker with ice. Strain into a cocktail glass with ice, serve with a lemon wheel or rind, and enjoy. This refreshing cocktail is sure to see a happy grin on your face.

FUN FACT

The Queen has herself, personally, held over 540 investitures and has met approximately 4 million people face-to-face.

> "In the words of one of my more sympathetic correspondents,
> it has turned out to be an 'annus horribilis.'"
> Queen Elizabeth II, speaking about the year 1992

Long To Reign Over Us

- 1 generous measure gin
- 1 measure apple juice
- 1 measure apricot brandy
- ½ tsp lemon
- lime wheel or rind, to garnish

Method: Stir (or shake vigorously for a fully mixed and frothy cocktail) all ingredients in a shaker with ice. Strain into a cocktail glass with ice, serve with a lemon wheel or rind, and enjoy. You will be all smiles after repeating the steps several times within a few hours.

FUN FACTS

During her reign, The Queen has journeyed on over 256 official overseas visits to 129 different countries.

The Queen has a bank account at Coutts & Co. There is a Coutts cash dispensing machine in Buckingham Palace.

The Crown Jewels

- 1 measure gin
- 1 measure Green Chartreuse
- 1 measure sweet vermouth
- 2 dashes ANGOSTURA® orange bitters
- cherry, to garnish

Method: In a shaker or pitcher, stir all ingredients and pour over ice in a small rocks glass. Garnish with cherry. This cocktail is smooth yet refined, a tribute to our Queen, and has remained timeless through the years.

FUN FACT

Elizabeth II, when a Princess, collected clothing coupons for her wedding dress. Parliament collected their own personal allotment of clothing coupons and presented them to Princess Elizabeth as a collective wedding present, so that she could have a long train.

Her Majesty's Imperial State Crown is made up of 2,868 diamonds, 273 pearls, 17 sapphires, 11 emeralds, and 5 rubies.

The Crown Jewels are 140 royal ceremonial objects kept in the Tower of London, which include the regalia worn by British kings and queens at their coronations.

The Commonwealth

- 1 generous measure gin
- 1 measure apple brandy
- ½ measure apricot brandy
- lemon rind, to garnish

Method: Pour all ingredients in a shaker with ice and shake vigorously. Strain into a cocktail glass, and serve with an orange slice. If you are feeling posh, simply strain into a chilled Martini glass and garnish with a lemon rind.

FUN FACT

Her Majesty's childhood nickname was Lilibet, reportedly because she couldn't pronounce Elizabeth.

> "Therefore I am sure that this, my Coronation, is not the symbol of a power and a splendour that are gone but a declaration of our hopes for the future, and for the years I may, by God's Grace and Mercy, be given to reign and serve you as your Queen."
> Queen Elizabeth II

The Royal Cuppa

- 1 measure gin
- ½ measure Dubonnet
- lemon wheel

Method: In a fine bone china teacup, place a lemon wheel under cubes of ice and pour in the spirits. Simply enjoy this favourite of not only Her Majesty Queen Elizabeth The Queen Mother, but Her Majesty Queen Elizabeth II, the Diamond Queen.

FUN FACT

The year 1940 was one of the most devastating years of the Second World War. London experienced the start of the Blitz bombing. A young Princess Elizabeth emphasised the necessity of hope, stating: "We know in the end that all will be well," she said as she made her first public address at the age of 14 on 'The Children's Hour', a BBC radio broadcast.

The Sandringham Sip

- 3 measures gin
- ½ measure dry vermouth
- green olive, to garnish

Method: Pour all of the ingredients (except the olive) into a shaker almost filled with ice. Shake vigorously and strain into a chilled Martini glass. Garnish with the olive and enjoy this most classic and famous of gin drinks. It is what we British are known for.

FUN FACT

During her reign, The Queen has received many unusual gifts, including a variety of live animals. The more unusual animals have been placed in the care of London Zoo, among them jaguars and sloths from Brazil and two black beavers from Canada. The Queen has also received gifts of pineapples, eggs, a box of snail shells, a grove of maple trees and 7 kg of prawns.

Royal Rum Drinks

"There's nought, no doubt so much the spirit calms as rum and true religion."

Lord Byron (1788 - 1824), English Poet

Like a child to a sweet shop, so are adults to rum - Yum! Sugar is sweet and born from the same element. Both of these smooth and delicious spirits are made simply by distilling water together with fermented sugar, which is from pure sugar cane. Most of the world's rums are the product of molasses which is the by-product of boiling sugar cane and extracting the crystallised sugar. Molasses is also used for more than distilling alcohol. Colonial sugar mill operators are credited with the discovery of molasses. They noticed that when sugar was mixed with water and left out on its own in the sun, the mixture would ferment. It was during the 1650s that this newly found product was used to distil alcohol. In our Caribbean colonies, rum was known as 'Kill Devil' (as it was known to give those who imbibed too much, intense hangovers), or 'Rumbullion' which was shortened to the term we know now.

In our colonies where rum was produced, it was often referred to as a medicine to cure all that ails the body. It was mainly used to treat aches and pains for those living in the Caribbean and throughout the tropics. Rum was inexpensive to manufacture and quick to produce. This enabled the sugar plantation owners to sell it at a heavily discounted price, which attracted passing naval ships to the area to purchase the alcohol. These visits would help discourage pirates that would often prey on the wealthy sugar plantations. It was not long before the British Royal Navy (in the 1730s) adopted a daily ration of a half-pint of 160 proof Rum. This ration of pure distilled rum was further modified by mixing it half and half with water to produce a distinct drink called 'Grog'. This maritime concoction continued to remain a staple of the British Royal Navy until 1969. As rum was sold to Navy ships and their sailors, it was not long before this alcohol was presented to the world beyond the Caribbean. By the turn of the eighteenth century, rum was a commodity that formed a new export for trade.

The British island colonies in the Caribbean produced and shipped rum home to not only Great Britain but to our other colonies, such as North America. Rum became so popular and it was during this time that it was made into punches and other related drinks which overtook gin in popularity.

The exporting of rum to our North American colonies (eventually the United States and Canada) in exchange for lumber and dried cod from New England eventually gave way to the export of raw molasses to newly-founded distilleries in North America, which helped avoid British taxes and laws which were implemented by Parliament. It was illegal at this time to trade spirits directly between the colonies, as doing so would prove damaging to British distillers. However, this law did not stop the illegal smuggling of rum. To this day, the trade of rum is very much alive and well, as Canada's 300-year-old tradition of trading rum for dried cod fish continues in the maritime provinces. The peoples of Nova Scotia and Newfoundland trade their goods in favour of importing golden rums from Antigua, Barbados and Jamaica. Europe today is primarily a blender of imported rums, where both Britain and France continue to import rums from the former Caribbean colonies for aging, bottling and selling.

The product of molasses consists of over 50 per cent sugar and is high in other elements and minerals that help contribute to the flavour of rum. There are several varieties and types of rum, but one must know that the choice of stills does have a significant effect on the final product. As rum is distilled, it is naturally a clear translucent spirit. It is the addition of caramel colouring and the length of barrel aging that gives it its heavy or light appearance. As rum is a natural product, so is the colouring that is used, as caramel colouring is but burnt sugar. Heavy rum and light rum are distinguished by the distilling processes used in their manufacturing. Lighter rums are purified and blended several times whilst being produced in column stills. Light rums are so named as they are 'charcoal filtered' and aged in oak casks which add to a smooth flow on the palate. Many of the world's light rums have little flavour or smell which closely resemble another clear alcohol - vodka.

Heavier rums differ from their lighter counterparts in that they are distilled in pot stills. This form of distilling heavy rums is very similar to the processes used to produce cognacs and Scotch, due to the fact that the pot stills are less "efficient" than column stills. Due in part to this difference, it is the extra-naturally produced additives such as fusel oils and flavours that add to the overall flavour of the rum. Like other alcohols, several brands of rum are produced by blending both light (column distilled) and heavy (pot distilled) rums to create a specific flavour and brand. Rums made from cane juice, such as those from the island nations of Haiti and Martinique, have a naturally smooth palate due in part to the distilling process in which the particular cane juice is fermented with airborne wild yeast or a cultured yeast for specific amounts of time. Light rums are aged for as little as one day and up to several weeks to create a full and heavy rum. Rum can be broken down into several classifications which are: Añejo, Dark, Gold, Light, Spiced and Flavoured.

Añejo rum refers to age-dated rums which are from different batches. These are blended together to create a distinct flavour of a brand from year to year. These rums will often be labelled with the age of the youngest rum used to mix the particular blend, whereas a handful of French-producing islands label their bottles with the date of vintage.

Dark rum lends its name to the certain colour of the rum, such as brown rum, black rum and red rum. This class of rum is darker than gold rum as it is aged longer in their charred oak barrels. Dark rums have a much stronger flavour than their lighter counterparts, as they have a distinct trace of spices with a heavy flavour of molasses and caramel colour. Dark rum is heavy-bodied and is most commonly used for drinking straight up as well as for use in mixed drinks and cooking. It is mainly produced on the island nations of Jamaica, Haiti and Martinique, although two of the most popular and award-winning dark rums are products of Central America, not the Caribbean. These two nations, Nicaragua and Guatemala, produced the award-winning Flor de Caña and Ron Zacapa Centenario.

Golden rums are commonly referred to as amber rums, which are darker that light rums in colour but not as dark as fully-fledged dark rum. Golden rums are found to be medium-bodied and are aged for several years in their oak casks which enhances their smoothness on the palate. Golden rums are normally aged in charred white oak barrels which are usually the by-product from the aging of Bourbon (whisky). These rums have more of a distinct flavour to them and are stronger than silver rums, but not as strong as their darker counterparts.

Light or white Rums are generally of a light-bodied composition. Usually clear in colour, they are known to have very little flavour. When light rums are aged in casks, the rum is then usually filtered to remove any impurity, such as colour. This process helps create a distinct palate which is extremely smooth. White rums are used mostly as mixers which are known to blend well with fruit flavours. Many rum punches are created and served with fruit juices that are very popular in resort areas of the Caribbean.

Spiced rums are known to be dark in colour and use the same base and process as its gold rum cousin. The spiced flavour of these rums are due to the addition of spices such as aniseed, cinnamon, rosemary and pepper as well as the caramel colour that is used in the distilling process. Some spiced rums are quite dark whereas cheaper varieties of this spiced favourite are based from white rum which has been darkened by artificial means.

Flavoured rums are fairly new to the alcohol market as a handful of manufacturers have started infusing their rum with hints of fruit flavours. This variety of rum is usually less than 40 per cent alcohol and is used to enhance mixed drinks or to sip cold, over ice, as a light refresher on hot days. The most popular flavoured rums on the market today are orange, coconut, lime, banana and mango.

Rum is not to be misunderstood as a cheap and lessened version of its other alcohol-based cousins. As with other sipping spirits such as cognac and Scotch, rum too has a distinct market and demand for its premium and super-premium blends. Such rums are produced and aged with the utmost of care. They have a bolder body and stronger flavour than other rums and are produced to be drunk in their virgin form. Like premium rum, over-proof rum is distinctive in the rum family. This type of rum has a much higher content than the standard 40 per cent rating. In fact, most over-proof rums consist of levels which are in excess of 60 per cent alcohol and have even been produced in the range of 75 to 80 per cent alcohol which is not uncommon in this finely-distilled sugary sweet liquid candy.

The Duke of Normandy

- 1 tbsp grenadine
- 1 tsp orange Curaçao
- 1 tsp lemon juice
- ½ measure rum
- ¼ measure brandy
- orange twist, to garnish

Method: In a shaker half-filled with ice, add all ingredients and again put on your winter gloves. Shake vigorously until frost appears on the outside of the shaker. Strain into a cocktail glass and serve with an orange twist.

FUN FACTS

Her Majesty is known as The Duke of Normandy in the Channel Islands.

With the birth of Prince Andrew at Buckingham Palace in 1960, Her Majesty became the first reigning sovereign to have a child since Queen Victoria, who had her youngest child, Princess Beatrice, in 1857.

The Queen hosted the first women-only event "Women of Achievement" at Buckingham Palace in March 2004.

Sandringham Sizzle

- 3 measures Demerara Rum
- ¾ measure lime juice
- ½ measure simple syrup
- 3 heavy dashes AGOSTURA® bitters
- fresh mint, to garnish

Method: In a tall glass filled with crushed ice, add the above contents including the leftover lime from which the juice was squeezed. Top off the glass with more crushed ice and, using your favourite swizzle stick, swizzle until the glass is cold. Serve with mint leaves and a large straw for easy drinking.

FUN FACT

In 1969, the first television film about the ordinary family life of The Queen and the Royal Family was made. It aired on the eve of the Investiture of Prince Charles as The Prince of Wales.

"I have to be seen to be believed."
Queen Elizabeth II

Prom at the Palace

- 2 measures light rum
- ½ tsp grenadine
- ½ juice fresh squeezed lime
- twist orange peel, to garnish

Method: In a mixing glass filled with ice, combine the rum, grenadine and lime juice, then swizzle until the mixture is equally distributed. Garnish with an orange peel and enjoy the evening!

FUN FACT

The Queen sat for the first and only hologram portrait in 2003.

"I declare before you all, that my whole life, whether it be long or short, shall be devoted to your service and the service of our great imperial family to which we all belong."
Queen Elizabeth II

The Caribbean Queen

- 1 ½ measure raspberry rum
- ½ measure dark rum
- ¼ oz 151% proof rum
- 1 ½ oz pineapple juice
- 1 ½ oz orange juice
- 1 oz Sweet & Sour Mix
- orange slice or lemon wheel, to garnish

Method: In a Hurricane glass filled with ice, mix all ingredients and stir until well-blended. Serve as is with an orange slice or a lemon wheel. For an added kick, add a floater of rum to the top of the drink (simply add a shot of rum on top of the drink and do not mix). Enjoy!

FUN FACT

Her Majesty was confirmed on 28th March 1942 in the private chapel at Windsor Castle.

"Oh dear, I hope it wasn't anyone important."
Queen Elizabeth II

Royal Mustique

- ¼ measure coffee liqueur
- ½ measure dark rum
- ½ measure coconut liqueur
- ¼ oz 151 proof (high proof) rum
- juice of ½ lemon
- 4 oz pineapple juice
- strawberry and/or cherry, to garnish

Method: In a mixing glass filled with cubed ice, add all ingredients and shake until frothy cold. Pour into a collins glass filled with cracked ice and garnish with a cherry and/or strawberry for added colour and flavour. This wonderful cocktail will transport you to the white sandy beaches of the Caribbean, if you have more than just a couple!

FUN FACT

Princess Margaret, Her Majesty's sister, received a plot of land on the island of Mustique as a wedding present from Colin Tennant (rumoured to be her suitor).

Her Majesty sent her first tweet in 2014 at the Science Museum, London.

In 2000, she sent her mother, Queen Elizabeth The Queen Mother, a telegram to mark her 100th birthday.

Montserrat Majesty

- 2 measures light rum
- 2 measures dark rum
- 2 measures passion fruit juice
- 1 measure orange juice
- juice of ½ lime
- 1 tbsp simple syrup
- 1 tbsp grenadine
- orange slice, to garnish
- cherry, to garnish

Method: In a large shaker, squeeze the juice from the lime over ice and continue to add the rest of the ingredients. Shake long and hard until the mixture is of a frothy cold consistency (you should be a pro at this by now). Strain into a Hurricane glass which will be garnished with an orange slice and a cherry which will complete this tropical refresher.

FUN FACT

The Queen has sat for approximately 140 official portraits during her lifetime, two of which were with The Duke of Edinburgh. Her Majesty was just seven years old when she sat for her first portrait in 1933, which was commissioned by her mother and painted by the Hungarian artist Philip Alexius de László.

St. Lucia's Lilibet

- 1 measure rum
- ½ measure coconut rum
- pineapple juice
- orange juice
- splash of Campari

Method: This recipe is simple and quick. Simply pour equal parts orange and pineapple juices into a large glass filled with ice, add in the rum and colour it red with Campari. Swizzle until the mixture is even in colour. Sit back and enjoy this delightful, light and refreshing cocktail.

FUN FACTS

An important innovation during The Queen's reign was the 1962 opening of The Queen's Gallery at Buckingham Palace to display items from the Royal Collection. Established by The Duke of Edinburgh, the new Queen's Gallery occupied the space of the Palace's bomb-damaged private chapel.

The Queen, who allows Parliament to convene in the Royal Palace of Westminster (Houses of Parliament), is not allowed to enter the House of Commons since she is not a member.

Her Majesty The Queen and HRH Charles, The Prince of Wales at Trooping the Colour.
Photo: Thomas J Mace-Archer-Mills.

Jamaican Queen

- 2 measures rum
- 1 tsp sugar
- ½ lime
- soda water
- lime slice, to garnish

Method: In a highball glass, mix all ingredients together and swizzle until the sugar dissolves. Add ice and top off with soda water. Simply garnish with a lime slice and enjoy the company you are with, be it with a group of friends or your new friend, the Jamaican Queen.

FUN FACT

The first football match The Queen attended was the 1953 FA Cup Final.

"I cannot lead you into battle. I do not give you laws or administer justice but I can do something else - I can give my heart and my devotion to these old islands and to all the peoples of our brotherhood of nations."
Queen Elizabeth II

Royal Scotch Drinks

presented in part by

By appointment to Her Majesty The Queen
Scotch Whisky Blenders
Matthew Gloag & Sons Ltd
Perth

Royal Scotch Drinks

"For God's sake, bring me a large Scotch..."
Reginald Maudling (1917 - 1979), British Politician

For the person who states that whisky is whisky, how acutely unaware they are of this finely distilled spirit. Out of all the whiskies in the world, Scotch whisky is by far the most notable, smooth and popular. There are only two basic types of Scotch from which all blends are made, namely single malt and single grain. Single malt is made from only water and malted barley which is distilled in pot stills at one single distillery. Single grain, however, is produced at one single distillery, but may have other additives to its distilling process, such as grains of other malted or unmalted cereals. Single grain, by definition, does not mean that only one type of grain is used in production, but that a single distillery is the venue for its production. Blended Scotch produced from single malt and single grain distilled at the same distillery are not to be confused, as there is a vast difference in their distillation process.

There are actually more blends that are made and defined by the term 'Scotch'. Blended malt Scotch whisky means a blend of two or more single malt Scotch whiskies from different distilleries. Blended grain Scotch is comprised of two or more single grain Scotches from different distilleries rather than one single distillery. Blended Scotch is a blend of one or more single malt Scotches with one or more single grain Scotches.

A whisky is subject to a very stringent set of rules set before it can be termed Scotch. New regulations in 2009 changed the formal definition of Scotch in a way that reflected both the traditional and current practice of distilling. Before the regulation changes (SWR) in 2009, any combination of Scotch qualified as Blended Scotch. This also included single malt Scotch.

The Scotch Whisky Act of 1988, SWR 2009 (provision 5) states that the only whisky that is allowed to be produced in Scotland is Scotch. In defining the term 'made' or 'manufactured' (as per the official term), the regulations state that manufacturing is "keeping for the purpose of maturation; and keeping, or using, for the purpose of blending, except for domestic blending for domestic consumption". By regulating to this extreme, this regulation prevents the existence of two grades of Scotch that would be a derivative of Scotland, Scotch Whisky and Whisky defined as a product of Scotland. The Scotch Whisky Association continues to protect the production of 'Scotch' by passing regulations that make it difficult for other whiskies that would be made in Scotland to be a distinctive product of Scotland, much like Scotch. Regulations passed prohibit any whisky production in Scotland that is not defined as Scotch as well as prohibiting the blending and maturing of whisky in Scotland that does not adhere to the distilling process set forth by the Association. The Scotch Whisky Association continues to help Scotch remain a distinct product of Scotland without imitations capitalising on the hard work and history of true Scotch whisky.

Around 90 per cent of the Scotch (whisky) produced in Scotland is a blend which contains both malt and grain whisky. Famous Scotch producers, such as Ballantine's, Chivas Regal, Cutty Sark, Dewars', J&B, Johnnie Walker and the Famous Grouse, all combine various malt and grain Whiskies in the production of their individual and distinctive style and brand.

Rule Britannia

- 2 measures Scotch
- 1 measure Drambuie
- 1 tbsp honey
- 2 tbsp lime juice
- lemon twist, to garnish

Method: In a mixing glass, combine all ingredients and shake until the honey is fluid. Pour into a rocks glass filled with ice and garnish with a lemon twist.

FUN FACT

The Queen has launched nearly 25 ships in her lifetime. The first was HMS Vanguard which she launched, as Princess Elizabeth, on 30th November 1944 in Clydebank. The first ship which she launched as Queen was Her Majesty's Yacht Britannia which was also launched from Clydebank. The last ship she named was Cunard's Queen Elizabeth in October 2010.

"It's all to do with the training: you can do a lot if you're properly trained."
Queen Elizabeth II

Balmoral Castle

- 1½ measures Scotch
- 1 measure sweet vermouth
- 3 dashes ANGOSTURA® orange bitters
- green olive, to garnish

Method: Stir (or shake vigorously for a fully mixed and frothy cocktail) all the ingredients in a shaker with ice. Strain into a Martini glass, garnish with the olive, savour and enjoy.

FUN FACTS

Since 1952, The Queen has undertaken approximately 112 State Visits accompanied by The Duke of Edinburgh, the last being to the Republic of Ireland in 2010 in which she is the first reigning British monarch to visit since Ireland gained independence in the 1920s.

In 1992, The Queen issued a writ against The Sun newspaper after it published the full text of her Christmas broadcast two days before transmission. She later accepted an apology and a £200,000 donation to charity.

The Birkhall Blend

- 1 ½ measures Scotch
- ½ measure Triple Sec
- 1 oz orange juice
- orange slice, to garnish

Method: In a shaker half-filled with ice, combine all of the ingredients and shake well – that's right... until frosty cold. Strain into an old-fashioned glass half-filled with ice cubes and garnish with an orange slice. Enjoy this alternative way of consuming vitamin C.

FUN FACTS

The Queen has given out approximately 80,000 Christmas puddings to staff continuing the custom of King George V and King George VI. In addition, The Queen gives all her staff a gift at Christmas time.

When The Queen was a young girl, she received tuition from her father, as well as sessions with Henry Marten, the Provost of Eton. She was also instructed in religion by the Archbishop of Canterbury.

The Palace of Holyroodhouse

- 1 ½ measures Scotch
- ½ measures sweet vermouth
- 2 tsp Bénédictine Liqueur
- 2 tsp grenadine
- cherry, to garnish

Method: Stir (or shake vigorously for a fully mixed and frothy cocktail) all ingredients in a shaker with ice. Strain into a rocks glass filled with ice, or to smarten up, make sure the shaker is frosty and strain into a Martini glass. Garnish with a cherry, savour, enjoy and make another.

FUN FACTS

The Queen learned to drive in 1945 when she joined the Army.

Since 1952, The Queen has given royal assent to more than 3,500 Acts of Parliament.

The Palace of Holyroodhouse is set in approximately 10 acres, which are part of the much larger Holyrood Park, and features gardens laid out by Prince Albert. There are 289 rooms in the palace. The largest room is the Great Gallery which is 44.5 metres long. The palace has 387 windows and 51 clocks.

The Royal Standard

- 1 ¾ measures Scotch
- ½ measure wine-based aperitif
- ¼ measure Drambuie
- 2 dashes sugar syrup
- orange slice, to garnish

Method: In a rocks glass half-filled with ice, add all ingredients and stir until your fingers are sore. Strain into a small snifter and garnish with an orange slice. Perfection in a glass!

FUN FACT

The Queen became a Girl Guide in 1937 and a Sea Ranger in 1943.

"We are a moderate pragmatic people, more comfortable with practice than theory."
Queen Elizabeth II

The Scots Guard

- 1 tsp powdered sugar
- ½ lemon
- 2 splashes ANGOSTURA® bitters
- 1 measure Scotch
- 1 oz sweet vermouth
- ginger ale

Method: In a mixing glass, add all ingredients, with the exception of the ginger ale, and give it a few good strong shakes. Pour into a rocks glass filled with ice and top off with ginger ale. Repeat these steps until your vision becomes blurry.

FUN FACTS

Her Majesty, as Princess Elizabeth, travelled on the London Underground for the first time in May 1939 with her governess Marion Crawford and her sister, Princess Margaret.

In 2010, when Her Majesty visited Wimbledon's Centre Court Royal Box to watch Andy Murray play, it marked the end of her 33-year absence.

Princes William and Charles in their robes of the Most Noble Order of the Garter.
Photo by Thomas Mace-Archer-Mills.

The Order of the Thistle

- 1 measure Scotch whisky
- ½ measure Peach Schnapps
- 1 measure blue Curaçao
- 3 measure grapefruit juice
- ½ measure lemon juice
- lemon twist, to garnish

Method: Stir (or shake vigorously for a fully mixed cocktail) all ingredients in a shaker with ice. Strain into a Martini glass rimmed with flavoured sugar crystals. Serve with a lemon twist and savour the flavour.

FUN FACT

Every year, The Queen sends Christmas trees to Westminster Abbey; Wellington Barracks; St Paul's Cathedral; St Giles' Cathedral, Edinburgh; The Canongate Kirk, Edinburgh; Crathie Church; and local schools and churches in the Sandringham area.

> "Like all the best families, we have our share of eccentricities, of impetuous and wayward youngsters and of family disagreements."
> Queen Elizabeth II

The Royal Mile

- 1 ½ measure Scotch
- ½ measure blue Curaçao
- ½ measure White Crème De Cocoa
- ½ measure white chocolate liqueur
- white chocolate shavings, to garnish

Method: In a mixing glass filled with ice, pour ingredients over ice and shake two to three times. Pour the mixture into a chilled Martini glass and serve with white chocolate shavings. Highly recommended for those with a sweet tooth.

FUN FACT

The Royal Mile is actually built on the side of an extinct volcano that leads to Edinburgh Castle. The charming narrow streets running down off the Royal Mile used to be some of the dirtiest streets in the city. Following the Royal Mile's slope downwards, one will be heading towards what used to be considered the World's End. This was the area outside the city wall (the rather silly sounding Flodden's Wall), which was a den of thieves and other nasty people you didn't want to come across late at night. The Palace of Holyrood House was opposite the other side of this sketchy area, but they didn't purposely put the palace somewhere 'up-and-coming' – Holyrood was unoccupied for a long time starting in the early sixteenth century.

St Andrew's Elixir

- 1 ½ measure Scotch whisky
- ½ measure sweet vermouth
- ½ measure dry vermouth
- 2 dashes ANGOSTURA® bitters

Method: In a mixing glass filled with ice, shake long and hard and immediately strain into a cocktail glass filled with ice cubes. Enjoy – it's that simple!

FUN FACT

Her Majesty is a keen photographer and enjoys taking photographs of her friends and family. The Duke of York is also a keen photographer and has taken a number of photographs of The Queen, including an official photograph for Her Majesty's Golden Jubilee in 2002.

"In tomorrow's world, we must all work together as hard as ever if we're truly to be United Nations."
Queen Elizabeth II

Royal Vodka Drinks

"There's no absolutes in life - only vodka."
Mick Jagger (1943 - present), musician, The Rolling Stones

It was during the days of 'Red America' that contemporaries 'modernised' the Martini as well as several drink recipes with the introduction of vodka. This mainly Eastern European spirit was rarely ever imbibed from the European continent before the 1950s; however sales of vodka in America topped that of bourbon by 1975. Progressing through the following years, vodka continued to rise in popularity, eventually being used in favourite drinks such as Bloody Marys, Screwdrivers, several Martinis etc. Vodka began to replace gin in Martinis along with several cocktails, soon becoming a favourite in bars as well as in the societies that frequented them. According to the Gin and Vodka Association, vodka was first distilled in 1174 at Khylnovsk, Russia as reported by the Vyatka Chronical, though scholars debate that it could have been distilled as early as the ninth century.

Vodka is produced by distilling fermented products such as grains, fruits, potatoes and sugars. Today's most popular vodkas are produced from grains including, but not limited to, corn, rye and wheat, whereas other forms of vodka are made from distilling grapes, molasses, potatoes, sugar beets and sometimes from odd resources such as wood pulp and by-products from oil refining. As one of the world's most favoured spirits, vodka in its traditional form possessed an alcohol content of 38 per cent by volume, whereas modern vodka sees a 40 per cent alcohol by volume (ABV) in nations such as Russia, Belarus, Poland, Ukraine and Lithuania. The European Union dictates an ABV of 37.5 per cent, whilst the United States dictates an ABV of 40 per cent or more in order for vodka to be named as such.

American and European vodkas are known for their extensive filtration techniques before processing and the incorporation of flavoured additives, whilst traditional techniques use precise and exact distillation methods with limited filtering, which preserves certain aspects and characteristics of its natural flavours. Filtering vodka is often completed in stills during and after distillation where the spirit can further be filtered through other items such as charcoal, which allows the absorption of alternative substances, and this can alter the flavour of vodka.

It is not uncommon for vodka to be distilled multiple times or distilled in a fractioning still, which not only improves the taste of the spirit but enhances its clarity. Water is vodka's main dilutive as the spirit is distilled until it is almost pure alcohol, where the water added determines the final alcohol content and flavour of the spirit, depending on origins of the water. There are two classifications of vodka: clear vodka and flavoured vodka, in which flavoured vodkas can further be classified in two categories: anniversary vodka and pepper vodka. Most vodka is unflavoured but flavoured vodkas are still produced in the same traditional way as their non-flavoured counterparts. Most times, flavoured additives, such as fruit flavouring, red pepper, ginger, chocolate, cinnamon and vanilla, helped mask the medicinal attributes of the spirit's natural flavour, such as vodkas made for medicinal purposes in the Ukraine which contained St. John's wort. Other such vodkas contain grasses, honey, spices, herbs and roots. This favoured, and often at times fruity-flavoured, spirit is traditionally drank neat in Eastern Europe which is traditionally known as the 'vodka belt'. It is also commonly used in various mixed drinks and cocktails, and the vodka tonic has often rivalled the gin and tonic as a favoured summer refresher.

St George's Chapel

- 2 measures vodka
- 1 measure Peach Schnapps
- 3 oz orange juice
- peach slice, to garnish

Method: In a collins glass filled with ice, add the ingredients and swizzle the mixture until evenly distributed. Garnish with a peach slice.

FUN FACT

In addition to racing, The Queen also takes a keen interest in horse breeding. Horses bred at the Royal Studs over the last 200 years have won virtually every major race in Britain. The Queen has about 25 horses in training each season.

"Work is the rent you pay for the room you occupy on earth."
Queen Elizabeth II

Admiralty Arch

- ½ measures vodka
- ½ measures gin
- ½ measure white tequila
- ½ measure light rum
- ½ measure Cointreau
- ½ measure lemon juice
- 4 measures Coca-Cola
- lemon wedge, to garnish

Method: Pour all ingredients (with the exception of cola and the lemon wedge) into a shaker almost filled with ice and shake vigorously until frothy cold. Strain the mixture into an ice-filled collins glass and slowly top off with cola. Garnish with the lemon wedge and indulge in this warming drink. A popular alternative to Afternoon Blend.

FUN FACT

In July 2002, Her Majesty visited a mosque for the first time in the UK whilst visiting Scunthorpe, Lincolnshire.

> "We lost the American colonies because we lacked the statesmanship to know the right time and the manner of yielding what is impossible to keep."
> Queen Elizabeth II

Gloriana

- 2 measures vodka
- 1 measure coffee liqueur

Method: Simply stated, pour the ingredients into a highball glass filled with ice and stir. If preferred, add ingredients into a shaker with ice and shake until frothy cold and strain into a rocks glass. There is not much to this recipe but to enjoy it for all its worth!

FUN FACT

Her Majesty continues the Royal Family's long association with racing pigeons. This tradition began in 1886, when King Leopold II of Belgium made a gift of racing pigeons to the British Royal Family. In 1990, one of The Queen's pigeons took part in the Pau race, coming first in the Section 5th Open and was subsequently named "Sandringham Lightning". In recognition of her interest in the sport, The Queen is Patron of a number of racing societies, including the Royal Pigeon Racing Association.

"I cannot forget that I was crowned Queen of the United Kingdom, of Great Britain and Northern Ireland. Perhaps this Jubilee is a time to remind ourselves of the benefits which union has conferred at home and in our international dealings on the inhabitants of all parts of this United Kingdom."
Queen Elizabeth II

HM Corgis

- 2 ½ measures vodka
- 4 measures grapefruit juice
- crushed sea salt
- lime wedge, to garnish

Method: To prepare this highball glass, rim the lip with a lime wedge and dip the glass into crushed sea salt, thus creating a salted crust on the glass. Add a few large ice cubes into the glass and pour the vodka and juice over the ice. Make sure to swizzle well and use the leftover lime wedge as garnish.

* Modify this drink by adding ¼ oz maraschino cherry liqueur, which will allow people who appreciate grapefruit juice to enjoy this drink without its usual bitter flavour. Brilliant!

FUN FACT

The Queen loves dogs and has owned over 30 corgis during her reign. Her first corgi, named Susan, was an 18th birthday present. In 2015, the Queen stopped breeding corgis so as not to leave any behind when she died. Her final corgi, Whisper, died on 26th October 2018. Her Majesty is also credited with creating a new bread of dog called a "dorgi" - a cross between a corgi and a dachshund. Her two dorgis, Vulcan and Candy, are still alive.

Bruton Street Belle

- 2 measures citrus-infused vodka
- ½ measure Cointreau
- ½ measure lemon juice
- ¼ lemon
- granulated sugar
- slice lime, to garnish

Method: In the shaker filled with ice, add the vodka, Cointreau and lemon juice. Shake vigorously until blended, and let sit for a few seconds to prepare the Martini glass. Rim the lip of the glass with a quarter of a lemon and dip it into the granulated sugar crystals, thus creating a sweet crust on the rim of the glass. Pour the frothy mixture from the shaker into the chilled and prepared glass and serve with a slice of lemon. This drink is guaranteed to prevent scurvy!

FUN FACTS

The Queen was born at 17 Bruton St, London W1 on 21st April 1926. She was christened on 29th May 1926 in the private chapel at Buckingham Palace.

At a fancy dress ball in her wedding year, Her Majesty dressed as a maid, whilst Prince Philip dressed as a waiter.

The Lady of London

- 2 measures lemon flavoured vodka
- ½ measure Cointreau
- ½ measure lime juice
- ½ measure cranberry juice

Method: Pour the ingredients into our shaker, which will be almost filled with ice. Shake it up like Parliament and Her Majesty's finances, and strain into a pre-chilled Martini glass. Imbibe quickly so as not to lose the chill of the drink. I highly suggest spacing out the consumption of this cocktail before you take to the cover of *Cosmo* like Burt Reynolds.

FUN FACT

The Queen does not purchase her hats from the High Street but has them made for her by milliners Frederick Fox, Philip Somerville and Marie O'Regan.

"My husband has quite simply been my strength and stay all these years and I owe him a debt greater than he would ever claim."
Queen Elizabeth II, Golden Wedding Anniversary speech, November 2007

The Glass Coach

- 2½ measures vodka
- 4 measures orange juice
- orange twist, to garnish

Method: In a tall slender cocktail glass filled with ice, pour the vodka and orange juice so that the ice is completely covered. Swizzle this mixture until evenly dispersed and add the orange twist as garnish.

FUN FACTS

Her Majesty's racing colours are: a purple body with gold braids, scarlet sleeves and a black velvet cap with gold fringe.

Her Majesty favours sheets and comforters in place of a duvet.

As a young girl, The Queen and her sister, Princess Margaret, acted in a number of pantomimes during World War Two, including playing the part of Prince Florizel in Cinderella in 1941. These pantomimes took place every year in the Waterloo Chamber at Windsor Castle.

In their early years, Princesses Elizabeth and Margaret were educated from home.

Bloody Queen Mary.

Bloody Queen Mary

- 2 measures vodka
- 4 measures tomato juice
- ½ measure lemon juice (some prefer lime juice)
- ¼ tsp ground black pepper
- ¼ measure Worcestershire sauce
- 1 dash Tabasco sauce
- 1 dash celery salt
- celery, medium stalk, to garnish

Method: In our trusty shaker, shake all of the ingredients (of course, we do not include the celery at this point) with ice until frothy cold. Continue by straining the mixture into a collins glass filled with ice and then add the celery stalk to the glass as garnish. This drink is perfect for the morning after you have imbibed the other drinks in this book, unless you have a keen feeling to know how Bloody Mary's (Mary I) prisoners felt whilst imprisoned in the Tower.

FUN FACT

Mary I is known as Bloody Mary for her persecution of Protestants: Mary abolished all religious legislation passed under Edward VI. Henry's religious laws were also repealed returning the English church to Roman jurisdiction. The laws against heresy were also revived. Over the next three years, hundreds of Protestants were burned at the stake. It is due to this that she became known as Bloody Mary. Her hopes of a Catholic England were ultimately shattered.

Royal Whisky Drinks

> *"A glass of whisky in Scotland in the thirties cost less than a cup of tea."*
>
> **Catherine Helen Spence (1825 - 1910),**
> **Scottish Author, Teacher, Journalist, Suffragette**

"To Friar John Cor, by order of The King, to make aqua vitae VIII bolls of malt." Exchequer Rolls 1494-95, vol x, p.487 - The Scotch Whisky Association has officially stated that the beginnings of whisky distillation are undetermined; however, it is known that the distillation of a similar spirit was performed by the ancient Celts. This Celtic spirit, known as Uisce or "water", eventually evolved into a form of whisky that we know today. Whisky distilling became prominent in the eleventh century at early Christian monastic sites and remained uninterrupted until 1644, when the Crown levied taxes on whisky production. This resulted in public outrage, leading people to take matters into their own hands by illegally distilling their own spirits.

King James IV of Scotland (1488 - 1513) was known to have a keen liking for whisky and granted a monopoly for the distillation of whisky to the Association of Surgeon Barbers. At this time, most of the distilling remained within the monasteries; however, between 1536 and 1541 King Henry VIII of England and Ireland dissolved the monasteries, forcing whisky production into private homes and onto farms. The process was fairly primitive; whisky was not matured and often drank as soon as it was distilled, resulting in a very raw and harsh taste on the palate.

HRH Prince Charles, The Duke of Rothesay tries his hand at stoking the famous peat kiln at Laphroaig Distillery.

Photo Credit: Laphroaig Whisky Twitter: @Laphroaig

It was not until the accidental discovery (when a person was dared to drink whisky from a forgotten cask), that whisky was found to be smoother and easier on the palate the longer it was aged. The Old Bushmills Distillery located in Bushmills, Northern Ireland, used this information and perfected the distillation process through "aging", and is often credited with being the oldest whisky distillery in the world, having maintained its distilling licence which was originally granted to Sir Thomas Phillips, a landowner and Governor of County Antrim, Ireland by King James I of England, VI of Scotland, in 1608.

The Act of Union, which united the Crown and lands of England and Scotland in 1707, saw a sharp rise in the tax of whisky. The English Malt Tax of 1725 saw most of the distillation of whisky in Scotland transformed into an underground movement. The Scots often hid their spirits under altars and in coffins so as to elude the government's representatives. In 1780, there were eight legal, but over 400 illegal distilleries! Parliament therefore passed an excise tax which lead to the easement of restrictions in legal distilleries, making it harder for the illegal production of whisky to remain profitable. The Excise Act, along with the introduction of a new distilling process in 1831 (the Coffey distillation process which produces a whisky that is smoother than before), and the destruction of wine and cognac production in 1880s France due to the Phylloxera bug, helped boost the popularity of whisky.

As whisky's popularity heightened, even the colonists in America could not turn a blind eye to it. It was during the war of American Rebellion that whisky was used both as currency and traded as a coveted commodity. Until a tax was levied against it, whisky was king in the eyes of the newly created American States. Between 1789 and 1794, tensions rose and the Whisky Rebellion took shape, climaxing in 1794 when over 500 people savagely attacked the fortified home of the American tax inspector. The taxes were eventually repealed in 1801.

In 2015, HRH Prince Charles, The Duke of Rothesay, visited the world famous Laphroaig Distillery on the Isle of Islay in Scotland's Inner Hebrides, to commemorate the 200th anniversary of the brand.

Photo Credit: Laphroaig Whisky Twitter: @Laphroaig

Whisky is consumed all over the world, but is mostly produced in grain-growing areas. Not all whisky is the same. There are many factors that set whiskies apart, such as the alcohol content, the base product and the quality of the product. For example, malt whisky is made from malted barley, whereas grain whisky is made from any type of grain. Blended malt whisky is comprised of a single malt from different distilleries, whereas pure malt or malt whisky is usually pure vatted, formerly called 'vatted malt whisky'. Single malt whisky is from one distillery that only uses one type of grain. If single malt whisky is described as a 'single cask whisky', it will contain whisky from several casks of different years which enhance the flavour and taste of the batch, and identifies which distillery it is from. The most notable of the distilleries that use this method, as well as indicating the processes associated with their specific distilling and maturing in a port wine cask, are Bushmills, Nikka and The Glenlivet.

Whiskies that are known to be blended whiskies are often made by mixing malt and grain whisky together with flavourings and caramel colouring. The whiskies that are simply described as Canadian, Irish or Scotch are blended whiskies from several distilleries so they are distinguished by a certain flavour, which also defines their brand, such as Canadian Club and Chivas Regal. Most blended whiskies rarely identify the distillery in which the brand was made; however, one blended whisky found in Ireland is known to come from only one distillery - Jameson Whiskey.

There is a distinct way in which whiskies are produced which leads to a division in quality and popularity. One such distinction between these whiskies is the cask strength of the whisky itself. Cask strength whiskies, which are also known as 'barrel proof', are quite rare and are often the most expensive. Barrel proof whisky is so named because it is bottled directly from the cask in its purest form. This allows the consumer to dilute the whisky to their own preferred taste, if dilution is necessary at all. Single cask whisky, which is also known as single barrel whisky, is often bottled by specialists in the field. These whiskies are bottled from a single barrel and are labelled from the individual cask from which they were bottled.

Single cask whiskies are often labelled with very specific information identifying the barrel itself as well as all associated numbers. Just because the brand of these whiskies may be the same, the taste of the whisky itself may differ due to different casks used and therefore the taste may not be consistent with a particular brand of single cask whisky.

Contrary to belief, whisky does not mature anywhere but in the cask. Therefore, even if the whisky sits bottled on a shelf for a long time, it is not getting better with age. The age of a whisky is determined by the amount of time the whisky has sat between distilling and bottling. What ages the whisky is the time that is has been exposed to the cask itself, which lends its efforts to the composition of the taste of the whisky. Although a bottle that has been around for a long time and has been unopened is usually thought to have a rarity value, it is no better than whiskies that have been bottled recently from a cask of a similar wood and time.

Whisky strengths average 40 per cent alcohol by volume, as is the minimum mandate in certain countries. However, the strength of whisky can and does vary, as it is known that cask strength whisky contains almost twice as much alcohol percentage than that of its counterparts. Currently, there are several nations that enjoy a healthy whisky production; English, Canadian, Irish, Scotch, Welsh and American whiskies rank amongst the most popular.

English whiskies have evolved and have again begun to be produced in great quantities. In late 2006, Norfolk became synonymous with single malt distilling, as St George's Distillery produced the first English single malt in over a century. Historically, it was the cities of Bristol and Liverpool that had gained fame as the centres of English whisky production and distilling.

Canadian whiskies are known to have a light and smooth style about them. It is a law in the Dominion of Canada that each so named "Canadian" whisky must be produced and aged in Canada using a base product of cereal grain, before aging in wood barrels no larger than 700L. Such whiskies may not be aged for less than three years to ensure the specific taste and quality expected of a Canadian whisky. Though noted for their rye whiskies, Canada does not use this grain in their production, as Canadian rye whisky is actually derived from corn.

Scotch whiskies are known to be distilled several times, anywhere from two times up to twenty times. Similar to Canadian regulations, Scotch must legally be aged for no less than three years in oak casks, markings on the bottle referencing its specific numbers as well as the age of the whisky which serves as a guarantee, henceforth the whisky is called 'guaranteed age whisky'. Scotch whisky is heavily regulated and only be called Scotch when distilled in Scotland. Scotch whisky of just "Scotch", is mostly comprised of malt and grain variations which are mixed together to create certain blends. The most defining aspect of Scotch is that some of the distilleries treat their malt with peat smoke to give it a very distinct smoked flavour. But not all famous Scotch whiskies use this in their whisky production. Wales has again entered the fold of whisky distillation. Operating the smallest distillery in the world, the Penderyn Distillery was the first distillery to open in 2000 since whisky production ended in 1894. Penderyn Single Malt Whisky is exported across the globe since first becoming available to the public in 2004.

Irish whisky is historically known to use pot stills in the distilling process of this normally triple distilled spirit. Column stills are also used in Ireland to produce grain whisky for blends. The most well-known types of whisky from Ireland are single malt, single grain, blended and pure pot still whiskies. Like their Canadian and Scottish counterparts, Irish whiskies must be aged for no less than three years, however, they are commonly aged three to four times more.

The Imperial State Crown

- 1 ½ measures whisky
- 1 measure Cointreau
- 1 oz Peach Schnapps
- ½ measure raspberry liqueur
- 1 measure raspberry juice
- 1 measure pineapple juice
- splash grenadine
- cherry, to garnish
- slice pineapple, peach, or raspberries, to garnish

Method: In a shaker filled with ice, pour in all ingredients and shake and shimmy until frost appears on the shaker. Strain into a Martini glass and serve with a cherry and a slice of pineapple, peach, or raspberries!

FUN FACT

When Her Majesty tires of talking to someone during an official or informal visit, she spins her wedding ring or switches her ever-present handbag from one arm to the other.

"And what do you do?"
Queen Elizabeth II, while knighting Premier League Chairman David Richards, November 2006

The Cross of St George

- 1 sugar cube
- 2-3 dashes ANGOSTURA® bitters
- 2 orange slices
- 3 measures whisky
- 1 oz grenadine
- maraschino cherry, to garnish

Method: In a shaker, dissolve the sugar cube with whisky by shaking until the cube has vanished. Add in ice and other ingredients and resume shaking. This should help build your arm muscles! Strain into an old-fashioned glass over ice, drink and make another.

FUN FACTS

Unbeknownst to Palace officials, an undercover British tabloid reporter managed to get work at Buckingham Palace in 2003. He said that The Queen used Tupperware containers to house her cornflakes.

A lesser-known interest of Her Majesty is Scottish country dancing. Each year during her stay at Balmoral Castle, The Queen gives dances known as Gillies' Balls, for neighbours, estate and Castle staff, and members of the local community.

The Queen's Flight

- 2 measures rye whisky
- ¾ measure sweet vermouth
- 1 measure absinthe
- ½ measure grenadine
- 2 dashes ANGOSTURA® bitters

Method: Stir (or shake vigorously for a fully-mixed and frothy cocktail) all ingredients in a shaker with ice, strain into a Martini glass (chips of ice should float in the drink), savour and enjoy.

FUN FACT

In 2007, Queen Elizabeth and His Royal Highness Prince Philip celebrated their 60th wedding anniversary – the longest marriage of any British monarch.

"Have you been playing a long time?"
Queen Elizabeth II to four British guitar greats,
Eric Clapton, Jimmy Page, Jeff Beck and Brian May,
at reception for British music industry at Buckingham Palace, March 2005

Welsh Guards

- 1 ½ measures rye whisky
- ¼ tsp maraschino liqueur
- 1 dash ANGOSTURA® bitters
- 1 tsp sugar
- 1 square of pineapple chunk
- 1 oz champagne, chilled
- lemon peel, to garnish

Method: In a mixing glass, add sugar and bitters and dissolve with a splash of water (or simple syrup). Continue to add rye whisky, maraschino and pineapple chunk, then top off the glass with ice and shake hard in order to crush the pineapple. Strain into a chilled cocktail glass and top up with champagne. Garnish with a lemon peel and enjoy!

FUN FACTS

The Welsh Guards (WG; Welsh: Gwarchodlu Cymreig), part of the Guards Division, is one of the Foot Guards regiments of the British Army. It was founded in 1915 by Royal Warrant of George V. The Welsh Guards Motto is: "Cymru am Byth" (Wales Forever).

Each morning, Her Majesty's breakfast table is laid out with porridge oats and cornflakes in Tupperware containers and yoghurt, along with light and dark marmalade.

The Queen's Diamond Jubilee Concert, The Mall, Buckingham Palace, 2012.

Party at the Palace

- 1½ measures blended whisky
- ½ measure light rum
- juice of ½ lemon
- 1 tsp powdered sugar
- carbonated water

Method: In a shaker, shake all ingredients (except carbonated water) with ice and strain into a highball glass over two to three ice cubes. Fill with carbonated water, stir, serve and enjoy this delightful experience. If you missed the Party at the Palace for Her Majesty's Golden Jubilee in 2002, where Brian May performed *God Save The Queen* from the roof of the Palace, then order the DVD, invite the friends around, make a few of these lovely drinks, and turn up the volume!

FUN FACT

The concert was held in the gardens of Buckingham Palace for the Golden Jubilee. The event was touted as the greatest concert in Britain since Live Aid, or possibly ever. Twelve thousand people attended the concert with an estimated one million people watching outside in The Mall and around the Queen Victoria Memorial, with 200 million more watching on television. The concert included performances of many hit songs from the reign of Queen Elizabeth II. The Party at the Palace was the culmination of a national day of partying.

"The Long Walk" and Windsor Castle
Windsor Great Park, Berkshire

The Long Walk of Windsor

- 2 measures Canadian whisky
- 1 measures sweet vermouth
- 2 dashes ANGOSTURA® bitters
- 2 dashes orange Curaçao

Method: In a shaker filled with ice, pour in all ingredients and shake until frost appears on the shaker. If you care to speed up the process, dance around with the shaker to your favourite song to pass the time to ensure ultimate frosting. Strain into a rocks glass filled with ice and serve. I can only suggest a long walk on a cold night after drinking several of these light cocktails.

FUN FACT

Windsor Great Park has been enjoyed by royalty since William the Conqueror's victory at the Battle of Hastings. It wasn't until William IV, however, that the Great Park, as we know it, was opened to the public, allowing visitors from far and wide to enjoy its splendour as they do today. Created by King Charles II, the nearly three-mile long "Long Walk" was introduced in 1680 – although it was not until 1683 that the avenue was extended to its current length. The iconic Copper Horse which stands guard over the Long Walk was also a later addition. This impressive statue, depicting King George III on horseback, was erected in 1831 to commemorate his significant contribution to Windsor Great Park.

The Maple Crown

- 2 measures whisky
- ¼ - ½ measure maple syrup
- 2 dashes ANGOSTURA® bitters
- ¼ - ½ measure Grand Marnier
- lemon twist, to garnish

Method: In a mixing glass, pour ingredients over ice and shake twice. Pour the mixture into a chilled Martini glass and serve with a lemon twist. After a few of these semi-sweet refreshers, Canada becomes closer to our hearts, and heads.

FUN FACTS

The Queen was the first British monarch to address a joint session of Congress in Washington, DC.

In 2010, Her Majesty The Queen delivered her Christmas address from Hampton Court Palace - the first time this historic building had been used.

The Maple Leaf

- 1 measure whisky
- ¼ measure lemon juice
- 1 tsp maple syrup

Method: Fill a shaker with ice and the aforementioned ingredients. Shake vigorously until hands are frozen (this creates a frothy head). Strain into a whisky glass and enjoy a true, strong and northern recipe for refreshment.

FUN FACT

The Canadian Red Ensign was the de facto national flag of Canada from 1868 until 1965 when it was replaced by the current maple leaf design.

"Are you a guitarist too?"
Queen Elizabeth II, to rock legend Eric Clapton regarding his guitar playing at Buckingham Palace reception for British music industry, March 2005.

The Royal Chocolate Biscuit Cake

A Royal Finale

Liquid Desserts

Nothing is complete without dessert or, as we say in Britain, pudding. Pudding is the finale to not just any meal I finish, but in your own households, and most importantly at Her Majesty's grand banquets which are held at Buckingham Palace and Windsor Castle. Just like those lucky enough to be invited guests of The Queen, we all certainly enjoy a decadent pudding course. However, I prefer my pudding to come in equal parts of liquid and solid form. Nowadays, puddings and aperitifs are the sweet component to any meal: breakfast, elevenses, luncheon, tea, dinner, supper and any snack which is perfectly paired with anything sweet. Sometimes, we even mix our favourite spirits with our favourite sweets to create the perfect pudding: one we can drink! Personally, I would prefer the pudding come at the start of dining rather than at the end, but then again, this is why I always save room for pudding, preferably in liquid form!

Dessert has historically been a great component of Royal dining and the most decadent of monarchs, King George IV, was very much the inventor of haute cuisine. His Majesty was known to feast, feast, feast, but his favourite part of dining was the sweet course. He is said to have not only enjoyed, but favoured the rich and decadent dessert known as Creme à la Carême, after his own celebrity French Chef, Marie-Antoine Carême. Queen Victoria enjoyed cake and sweets so much that Her Majesty used her own wedding cake in 1840 to make a romantically sweet statement. Victoria's love of sweets and extravagance were paired together to create a very specific request for her wedding cake; handmade orange flower blossoms and white icing, which covered the entire dessert cake, an idea which Catherine, Duchess of Cambridge, borrowed for her own wedding cake in 2011.

Sweets have always played a large part in British Royal history, but none so much as during the reign of King Edward VII. So great was His Majesty's love of chocolate, that he was the driving force between the match made in heaven of Madame Charbonnel and Mrs Walker. Together in 1875, these ladies created one of the best known and beloved British chocolatiers, Charbonnel et Walker, which not only happens to be my favourite chocolatier, but to this day, supplies chocolates to the Sovereign and her family. Chocolate was first introduced into Britain by King Charles II to compete with the French Court, but it was King Edward VII who helped create the most exquisite and luxurious chocolates within the nation. Alexandra, consort of Edward VII and daughter-in-law of Queen Victoria, was a hands-on and well experienced cook in her own right. She delighted in a sweet natural dessert consisting of red berries, thickened with potato starch and served with raspberry jelly and crème. This dessert, named Roodgrod, was brought with her from Denmark and was always a comforting delight for the Queen being so far from home.

Consorts to British kings and queens have come from a far, but not so far as King Edward VIII's American love, Wallis Simpson. Mrs Simpson was part and partial to Montego Bay Ice with a buttery rum sauce – a light and refreshing dessert that was a stark contrast to the dark and heavy clouds which shadowed her and the Duke of Windsor, leading up to and after their marriage. No matter how upsetting life may have seemed at times for Wallis, The Duchess of Windsor was never far from a smile when she would reach into a box of her favourite Charbonnel et Walker chocolates.

Pudding, or dessert as it is referred to in the Americas and in certain Commonwealth countries, can be either sweet or savoury. In the United Kingdom, pudding is referred to as a direct synonym to the dessert course, which this chapter will explore in depth and with an all liquid alternative. The word itself originates from the French "boudin" which is derived from the Latin "botellus" which means "small sausage". This "sausage" is a direct reference to the meats used in European puddings during the medieval age. Okay, most sausages are not sweet and one certainly would not think of eating a sausage for dessert, but please bear with me for this

delectable explanation. Puddings can be either sweet or savoury, to which depending on the country will dictate what it is that you are making or ordering. Dessert (sweet) puddings are quite rich and usually of a dairy or starch base such as rice pudding, crème brulee, treacle sponge pudding and our famous Christmas puddings. In the Americas, sweet milk-based puddings are referred to as custards or mousse. The savoury puddings which Britain is most famous for are "Yorkies" (Yorkshire pudding), black pudding, steak and kidney pudding, and several others. Sometimes, savoury puddings form part of a course, such as the main. Traditionally in Britain, Sunday roast is not to be missed and a Yorkshire pudding is served alongside the roast and vegetables. There are only a few "puddings" which would accompany a main course, with most beings consumed after as a sweet dessert.

Before dining courses became fashionable in the Court of nineteenth-century France, the British Court dined en-masse, eating meats with sweets which gave us our famed mincemeat. Over time, the meat was phased out, leaving us with what we have come to recognise as the sweet Christmas favourite: mincemeat. The holiday interim sees many sweets and desserts consumed, but none so much as chocolate. Everyone enjoys chocolate; milk, dark, white, flavoured etc. We enjoy hot chocolate, drinking chocolates, chocolate coffees, chocolate bars, chocolate bonbons, chocolate cakes, chocolate soufflés, chocolate mousse, chocolate biscuits, and the list goes on and on and on. However, there is one family and one person in particular who is quite fond of this sweet and luxurious blend of cacao, sugar and other ingredients – Her Majesty The Queen.

Though Her Majesty is not a great lover of many sweets, chocolate is certainly her addiction. Around the festive time of year, regularly around Christmas to be exact, a special shipment of only three to four small batches of a top secret and highly coveted Cadbury's chocolate recipe are supplied to the Royal Household for The Queen and her family to consume. This recipe is so extraordinarily secret, that we only know that it has been specifically engineered to the preferences of The Queen's own palate. These chocolate bars are made by a very small team of people, no more than three, on equipment at the Bournville, Birmingham factory, which is solely reserved for Royal manufacturing. When this special recipe of Royal chocolate is not being made, the equipment is covered and decommissioned until the Palace places another order. Once the Royal chocolate is made and poured into bar form, each bar is then specifically wrapped in gold foil and finished with a "Buckingham Palace" red wrapper, complete with Her Majesty's coat of arms. This special chocolate is simply referred to as "Royal Household chocolate" which is only delivered to Buckingham Palace, Windsor Castle and Sandringham House just before Christmas.

Her Majesty Queen Elizabeth The Queen Mother enjoyed her chocolates very much and this was recently reinforced with the 2010 film *The King's Speech*. In the award winning film, The Queen Mother is seen in the early scenes offering a little boy a chocolate "sweetie" whilst she is waiting for her husband to finish his speech therapy session. Later on, she is seen sitting in the back of a car being driven to Balmoral Castle with her husband, The Duke of York. The Queen Mother is pictured with a box of sweets on her lap which are similar in shape to the chocolate bonbons she was known to favour. At one of her friends' homes, Queen Elizabeth The Queen Mother giggled as a dog desperately tried to infiltrate her handbag. With a light laugh, The Queen Mother said, 'Perhaps she's sniffed out the chocolates... the corgis always sniff them out at Sandringham. At least one hopes it isn't the gin.' Her Majesty then reached into her handbag and drew out a linen handkerchief containing four Charbonnel et Walker rose-flavoured handmade chocolates. She continued, 'The blood sugar can get a little low at my age, but chocolates always do the trick. I haven't had a dizzy spell yet. Besides,' she added in her well known mischievous manner, 'it's nice to have a treat after an indifferent meal.' Perhaps one of the most famous desserts associated with this terribly sweet Royal is, "The Queen Mothers' Cake". This flourless cake was originally chosen to be made for The Queen Mother by eminent pianist Jan Smeterlin who was a close personal friend of hers.

When she ate this lovely baked delight, she asked him for the recipe, to which she then served it frequently to her guests at her numerous and lavish Royal dinner parties.

The sweet tooth of the Windsor family is long indeed, as successive generations of our Royal Family have come to inherit this sugary trait. Queen Mary had an insatiable sweet tooth and was known to always have a large box of chocolates positioned at her bedside. When she was visited by the younger royals, she was very generous with her sweets, offering them at will to her young relatives. As Queen Elizabeth II did not keep many sweets around Buckingham Palace, the children were always happy to make trips down the mall to visit Queen Mary, where they were always ensured a chocolate or two. Princess Elizabeth and Princess Margaret indulged in several sweets such as crisp chocolate-coated peppermint cremes, Charbonnel et Walker violet and rose chocolate cremes and barley sugar sweets which were kept in a glass jar on a side table in the drawing room. Princess Margaret enjoyed chocolates well into the course of her life, always preferring and demanding the best, which she considered Charbonnel et Walker. Princess Margaret's sister, The Queen, enjoys chocolate mousse so much that some Royal chefs have stated this to be one part of her favourite dessert, and that she just cannot resist its temptations. Chocolate Perfection Pie has been served not just after dinner, but also at luncheons held in honour of visiting heads of state and foreign diplomats. This Royal favourite possesses layers of chocolate mousse, layers of meringue and a layer of cinnamon cream, which Her Majesty still enjoys at 93 years of age.

Chocolate is loved by the Royals, especially Chocolate Biscuit Cake. This cake is a favourite staple of Her Majesty which she often enjoys with her afternoon cup of tea. Princes William and Harry have not only eaten, but made this cake during their childhoods. It was such an impressive sweet that Prince William served it as his groom's cake at his wedding to Catherine Middleton in 2011. His Royal Highness Prince William is also partial to something a little more natural such as banana flan. Both His grandmother The

Queen and the Prince enjoy this ripened classic. The Duchess of Cambridge Catherine enjoys sticky toffee pudding, even though she prefers healthy, organic foods, much like Princess Diana did. The Princess of Wales, though health conscious, always made room for her favourite bread and butter pudding – a British classic. The Princess' younger son, Prince Harry, is partial to golden treacle tarts. Harry was known to sneak into the Royal kitchens and regularly ask the chefs for this delicate treat. Knowing how much the little prince loved this dessert, the chef would keep a supply on hand for when His Royal Highness would make one of his frequent visits downstairs. In addition to Chocolate Biscuit Cake, Her Majesty enjoys the traditional Scottish Dundee cake. The Queen is said to enjoy this cake so much that she has reportedly travelled with the cake on several foreign tours, so that she would always have a familiar taste of home around tea time. Like his wife, Prince Philip, is known to like chocolate as well and is known to prefer a chocolate soufflé known as Andrassy Pudding.

It seems as if Princes William and Harry have taken after their father, Prince Charles, with their like of sweets. Like his father, Prince Philip, the Prince of Wales was enthralled with the workings of the kitchen, so much so that he would often visit the kitchens and offer his help to the working chefs. The Prince would often mix different ingredients together and experiment with recipes to create something unique to his person. As a child, Prince Charles enjoyed experimenting with and making recipes for ice lollies. He liked the ices so much that he even bought a plastic tray with sticks so that he could make several batches for himself. The young prince would often make his favoured flavours of orange and strawberry, but in the end chocolate remained his preferred sweet. Together with his sister, Anne, The Princess Royal, Prince Charles and the princess would often stock pile Kit-Kat bars so that they were never without their favourite sweet.

As we grow and mature, our palates and tastes change. As Her Majesty has turned to fruit to satisfy sweet cravings, preferring grapes to Prince Charles' lychees, many of us continue to enjoy the sweets we remember from our childhoods, whether they be manufactured or grown by mother nature. The Windsor family is able to enjoy the fresh fruits of their summer sojourn at Balmoral Castle by indulging in the sweet enhancement of nature's flavours. Here in Scotland, the Royal Family enjoys the fresh, ripe and sweet fruits, including strawberries, which grow during the summer months. Eton Mess is clearly a favourite dessert for the Royals, as such fresh fruits can be combined with meringue and whipped cream to create this light, yet sweet dessert, of which I too am a great lover of.

Keeping desserts light and sweet are important, especially those that come in liquid form. As we have explored the delectable and lavish confections and desserts which are preferred by the Royal Family, it is time for us to enjoy something a bit more refreshing and a little more alcoholic. With my love of puddings, chocolates and all things sweet, I am proud to welcome you to a dessert chapter unlike any other. A chapter which blends the very themes of this book together with the sweet and rich flavours that desserts, blended with spirits, provide. As we always crave something sweet and more times than not indulge in a bit more than we should, we must remember that the alternative desserts highlighted within this pudding chapter can impair more than your waist size. Do enjoy these dessert drink cocktails and please make sure that you pair each of them with upstanding confections that are truly decadent and luxurious, creating the best Royal dessert experience for you to enjoy.

Cocktails by Lorenz Tullio Santonocito

The Royal Chocolate Biscuit Cake

- 50 ml dark chocolate liqueur
- 10 ml blended rum
- 20 ml Cointreau
- three drops orange essence

Method: In that well used Martini shaker, which you should be very well familiar with, add the above stated ingredients over ice. Shake vigorously until ice chips have formed in the shaker. Strain directly into a crystal Martini glass and finish with orange zest.

Pair with a Dark Orange Fondant Chocolate, Milk Chocolate Orange Thins, or Fine Dark Chocolate Orange Sticks. These absolutely decadent chocolates make the perfect after treat to accompany such a wonderfully delicious cocktail.

FUN FACT

In 2013, Her Majesty received a chocolate model of Windsor Castle from the Mars chocolate company.

> *"All you need is love. But a little chocolate now and then doesn't hurt."*
> Charles M Schulz

The Royal Chocolate Mousse Martini.

The Royal Chocolate Mousse Martini

- 40 ml lavender chocolate mousse
- 20 ml dark rum
- 20 ml Yuzu gel
- cinnamon sticks, to garnish
- cherry to garnish

Method: You guessed it! In our faithful shaker, add the above ingredients and shake well. Double strain this mixture into a glass and garnish with a cherry.

Pair with a box of milk chocolate praline crowns or English dark chocolate mint thins - wafer thin discs of rich dark chocolate infused with the delicate taste of English mint. To be honest, any aforementioned chocolates from one of the four Royal Warrant Holders would pair exquisitely with this rich and luxurious dessert cocktail.

FUN FACT

Her Majesty's soft centre for chocolate is reflected in the warrants held by Charbonnel et Walker, Prestat, Cadbury and Bendick's, though Royal sales plummet in the 40 days before Easter, when the Queen abstains for Lent.

"The 12-step chocoholics program: Never be more than 12 steps away from chocolate!"
Terry Moore

HM Queen Elizabeth II in the Robes of the Most Noble Order of the Thistle.
Photo credit: Julian Caulder.

A Royal Lime and Raspberry Tarte

- 40 ml dry gin
- 4 drops ANGOSTURA® bitters
- 10 ml lime juice
- 10 ml Smoked water
- 10 ml raspberry liqueur
- red peppercorn beans, to garnish

Method: Build this tasty cocktail in a white wine glass. Gently swizzle the cocktail in the glass until well mixed. Finish with tonic and garnish with red peppercorn beans.

Pair with raspberry Marc De Champagne truffles, sea salt almonds, Crème Parisiennes or gin truffles. Gin truffles are not only my favourite but are a decadent addition to any after dinner experience. Most are made with London Dry Gin of truly uncompromising quality and character - simply divine!

FUN FACT

Petit fours are not considered a dessert, but a compliment to aperitifs or a long coffee.

"Dessert is to a meal what a dress is to a woman."
Béatrice Peltre

The Royal Violet and Hibiscus Drop

- 25 ml gin
- 25 ml dessert wine
- 10 ml lemon juice
- 10 ml violet liqueur
- 15 ml hibiscus liqueur
- violet flower, to garnish

Method: Once again, reach for that trusted Martini shaker. Add the above ingredients into the ice-filled shaker and shake very well. Strain the cocktail into a rocks glass over ice and garnish with a violet flower.

Pair with a box of fine Rose & Violet Creams – a favourite of our Royal Family. Rose & Violet Creams are a great British classic and are mostly infused with attar of roses and violets (the essential oil extracted from the petals).

FUN FACT

The Royal kitchens make a home-made vanilla ice cream for Her Majesty Queen Elizabeth II, which includes both double crème and clotted crème.

"Life's short. Eat dessert first, work less and vacation MORE!!"
Lea Mishell

A Royal Fiesta

- 50 ml white tequila
- 20 ml basil liqueur
- 15 ml Triple Sec
- 20 ml lime juice
- 4 basil leaves

Method: In a fresh Martini shaker with ice, combine the above ingredients and shake until well chilled. Double strain this mixture into a cut Crystal coupé. No garnish is necessary.

Pair with a box of Cocoa Dusted Almonds. Delicious Cocoa Dusted Almonds are whole almonds covered in milk chocolate and dusted with cocoa powder. So incredibly delightful they are, we know that you will keep wanting more well after this cocktail is finished.

FUN FACT

Describing his dessert of brandy snap cornets filled with ice cream, Royal Chef Darren McGrady ponders, "I think that is the closest The Queen ever came to eating ice cream out of a cone."

"I hope there's pudding!"
J.K. Rowling, *Harry Potter and the Order of the Phoenix*

The Duke and Duchess of Cambridge, Prince George and Princess Charlotte, Trooping the Colour, 2016. Photo: Thomas Mace-Archer-Mills.

The Royal Strawberry Patch

- 40 ml gin
- 10 ml strawberry liqueur
- 5 ml lemon juice
- 5 ml balsamic vinegar
- 2 fresh strawberries
- 4 basil leaves

Method: Muddle the strawberries with the lemon juice in the Martini shaker. Slap the mint a few times to release the aroma and oils and add to the shaker. After muddling and slapping, add 4 cubes of ice and the remaining ingredients to the shaker and shake vigorously. Double strain this cocktail into a frosted Martini glass and garnish with a strawberry and basil leaf.

Pair with a box of dusted Strawberry Truffles, filled with strawberry flavour and budding richness. The result of pairing this truffle to the decadence of the cocktail will result in an experience so delicious that you would think you were eating freshly picked strawberries!

FUN FACT

For rationing reasons, the cake for the 1947 wedding of Princess Elizabeth and Lieutenant Philip Mountbatten RN used "ingredients given as a wedding present by the Australian Girl Guides". The cake was baked by McVitie & Price.

"I've never met a problem a proper cupcake couldn't fix."
Sarah Ockler, Bittersweet

A Royal Relaxation

- 40 ml whisky
- 20 ml sweet vermouth
- 20 ml Amaro Averna liqueur
- 10 ml Campari
- 2 drops of ANGOSTURA® orange bitters

Method: In a mixing glass, stir in all of the above stated ingredients and swizzle with a few cubes of ice so as not to over chill the mixture. Strain this cocktail into a cut crystal coupé. Garnish with a twist of orange.

Pair with a box of Whisky Truffles. A deliciously dark chocolate truffle with a rich, dark chocolate ganache and Scotch whisky centre, lightly dusted in cocoa powder. One may also pair this cocktail with a box of Milk Orange Thins - Wafer thin discs of our finest Milk Chocolate blended with the taste of fresh oranges.

FUN FACT

A partiality for Chocolate Oliver biscuits was shared by the Queen Mother and John Lennon.

"Look, there's no metaphysics on earth like chocolates."
Fernando Pessoa

The Royal Banana Flan

- 40 ml blended rum
- 20 ml cognac
- 10 ml banana liqueur
- 4 drops chocolate bitter
- cinnamon stick, to garnish

Method: In our freshly washed and dried shaker, mix all of the above listed ingredients with ice and shake until ice chips are created within the mixture. Strain the cocktail into a cognac glass and garnish with a cinnamon stick.

Pair with a box of Sea Salt Almonds. These delicious almonds are coated in milk chocolate with a sea salt and cocoa powder dusting. One may also pair this luxurious cocktail with a box of fine dark chocolates.

FUN FACT

Sixty-five years on, the McVitie connection continues with chocolate biscuit cake, "without a doubt, the Queen's favourite tea cake". It contains 8oz McVitie's Rich Tea biscuits and 4oz of dark chocolate and is topped with another 8oz of dark chocolate.

> "There are two kinds of people in the world: those who love chocolate, and communists."
> Leslie Moak Murray

About the Author

Thomas Mace-Archer-Mills

Thomas Mace-Archer-Mills enjoying tea at Buckingham Palace on Grenadier Day 2013.

Thomas J. Mace-Archer-Mills is the Founder, Visionary and Chairman of both Crown & Country Magazine and of the British Monarchist Society. He is a Freeman of the City of London and Member of the Royal Society of St. George. Originally from New York, Thomas' professions in addition to the aforementioned are as a Royal Historian, Royal Consultant, Author and Educational Speaker.

Thomas has logged nearly 200 media credits to his name as a Royal commentator and media expert as an authority on the Royal Family, working with international media for nearly eight years. He has contributed to such publications as Majesty and Royalty Magazines, Political Pundits UK, The Conservative Blog, and Professor David Flints' "An Opinion Column from the National Convenor" in Australia. He has further appeared in print with BBC, The Times, Correio Barzilinese; WENN; The Daily Mail; The Daily Mirror; London Evening Standard; Newham Recorder; and many more. He has appeared on ITV3, BBC; BBC South East; BBC Radio 3; BBC Radio 4; BBC Radio Manchester; BBC

Radio Ulster 2's "Talkback"; CTV News; ARTE; Australia News 7; TF1's 50 Minutes Inside, repeatedly; Voice of American, Voice of Russia; NTV Russia; Polish Television and Radio; Australia Today; SRF, RS1; Arabia Television; and many other television outlets around the world.

Thomas is most recognised for his works in conceptualising and overseeing the creation and completion of the 2015 "Realms Portrait" for Her Majesty, The Queen, which was commissioned by the British Monarchist Society and gifted to her by the Commonwealth Realms at St. James' Palace in celebration of her becoming the Longest reigning Sovereign in British history on 9th September 2015, organising the Belgrade Royal Wedding of Prince Philip of Serbia in October 2017 and for his live commentary at the Royal Wedding of the Duke and Duchess of Sussex at Windsor Castle on 19th May 2018. Thomas has further been recognized for his contributions to "Lifeline" in New York, Crown Princess Katherine of Serbia's charitable foundation.

Thomas has further been a radio presenter for London's Wizard Radio, which is broadcast internationally, where he hosted several different shows with varying themes, for over five years. Thomas' last show was dedicated to helping the youth of the world overcome personal issues, challenges and negativity which faced the daily lives of his young listeners on "Therapy with Thomas Mills".

Thomas notably addressed the Annual General Meeting of the Australian Monarchist League in Sydney during the summer of 2015 and has lectured for Model Westminster and the Young Adults Forum in Parliament in the Autumn of 2016 and in the Winter of 2017. In honour of Her Majesty's Diamond Jubilee in 2012, Thomas penned his first book with permission of the Palace, to which he was granted the use of the official Diamond Jubilee logo. "To The Queen: A Royal Drinkology" went on to sell 5,000 copies in the months following the central Jubilee weekend. In his spare time (which is very limited), Thomas enjoys travelling, horseback riding, sailing, the arts, theatre, music, fine dining, reading and writing.

Thomas Mace-Archer-Mills with his grandfather, Grenadier Guard (Ret.) George Albert Mills.

HM Queen Elizabeth II and HRH Prince Phillip in the robes of The Most Noble Order of the Garter.
Photo: Thomas Mace-Archer-Mills.